COLLEGE
SMARTS

COLLEGE

SMARTS

The Survival and Success Guide

FOR CANADIAN STUDENTS

CATHERINE DOUGAN, M.SC.
DR. RON DOUGAN

REDSTONE

Co-published in 1998 by RedStone Publishing
1801-8 Street S.W., Calgary, Alberta, Canada T2T 2Z2
Tel. (403) 228-0880   Fax (403) 245-8725

and

Stoddart Publishing Co. Limited
34 Lesmill Road, Toronto, Canada M3B 2T6
Tel. (416) 445-3333   Fax (416) 445-5967

02 01 00 99 98 1 2 3 4 5

Canadian Cataloguing in Publication Data

Dougan, Catherine, 1940–
College smarts : the survival and success guide for Canadian students

ISBN 0-7737-6013-X

1. College student orientation — Canada — Handbooks, manuals, etc.
2. College students — Canada — Life skills guides.
3. Study skills — Handbooks, manuals, etc.
I. Dougan, Ron, 1930–   .   II. Title.

LB2343.34.C3D68 1998a   378.1'98'0971   C98-931466-9

Cover Design and layout: Gherkin Studios
Back cover photo: Dwayne Brown Studio Inc.

Printed and bound in Canada

*To our children: Jenny, Laura, David, Barbara, Janet, Leslie and Jonathan,
with whom we have walked this walk.*

*To our parents, Susanne and Wolfgang Fricke,
and to the memory of Nina Dougan Andrews and Harry Dougan,
whose love of learning and education was instilled and nurtured in us.*

Contents

Acknowledgements

Many people have participated in this book, and we thank them all. Most particularly, we owe gratitude to our youngest daughter, Jenny Grant, for her contagious optimism, patient reading, and insightful comments.

Gerald Smetaniuk guided us through early attempts at order, giving us the benefit of his outstanding project management skills. Our son, David Grant, taught us how to "zip" a manuscript, and produced copies of the first draft for our invaluable student reviewers. Whenever we had computer problems, Randal Penman and Les Dougan came to the rescue. They spent many hours coaching us in the mysteries of Microsoft, reassuring us that nothing was lost forever -- merely recycled. Our web page, which will allow us the opportunity to meet you on the internet, is designed and maintained by Debra Penman.

We owe a special note of thanks to the following students, for reading the manuscript and offering their comments, opinions and ideas, many of which appear on these pages: Meaghan Evans, Paul Fricke, Cindy Giesinger, Riley Gilchrist, Tammy Grant, Janne Holmgren, Heather Innes, Derrick McDougall, Arlin Pachet, Debra Penman, Randal Penman, and Mika Yamamoto.

Our publishers, RedStone Publishing, have been an energetic and vibrant team who encouraged us to believe in this book and in ourselves. Janet Alford, our editor, lifted our text to the next level with her fresh vision and understanding of our audience. She has managed this project with skill and a light touch. Ross Gilchrist took the initial idea and recognized its potential. He has continued to champion us. To Stoddart Publishing, who believe that this book is an important contribution to all Canadian students, we offer our thanks. William Hum designed the stunning book cover and reader-friendly page layout.

Our family and friends sustained, encouraged, and humoured us, even when our single-minded pursuit of this project might have become tedious to them.

Where would we have been without each other? Collaborating on this book, as we have done on so many of Life's projects, has been yet another loving experience of discovery and appreciation, both for each other and for our partnership.

Preface

"You should write a book."

This was music to our would-be writers' ears -- but only fleetingly. Almost immediately the "yes buts" clamoured. What would we write about? When would we find the time?

So the idea lay dormant, as we worked with students who wrote tests and explored career options; who agonized over entrance requirements, applications, courses, and finances; who debated The Best University Or College; who lived with too much work, too much confusion, not enough skills, too little time. At the end of a particularly challenging session with a student and his parents, painfully aware of how many times we had covered the same turf, the light dawned. We knew what we wanted to write. The passion took hold.

At the time, our youngest daughter was living at home and completing her undergraduate degree. She embraced our project with enthusiasm, adding immensely to the immediacy and relevance of our research and writing. Her student colleagues brought us their ideas and their fears, often leaving happily with problems solved or concerns validated. We heard a common lament from many of them: "I wish I could talk to my parents like this." As parents ourselves, we became aware again of how difficult it can be to talk to our children, and they to us, about important things in their lives. (We have often found it is one thing to be a professional counsellor with knowledge and expertise; it is quite another to be a parent with a vested interest in the choices and decisions.)

We questioned students, and parents, constantly. What would help in a book like this? What information was difficult to find? What resources were plentiful, and what were scarce? What did they do if they ran into trouble? How did they solve problems and what did they do to cope? When and how did they start planning for college? What were the most useful things they wished they could tell other students? That dialogue inspired our thinking and informed our writing.

In our ideal world, every potential post-secondary student will seek out, and thrive in, an educational experience which is right for them. To this end, we offer our contribution.

Introduction to Our Student Readers

The phrase *student readers*, we know, covers a lot of ground. Some of you are in Grade 10 or 11, beginning to think about what is perhaps the first major choice point in your lives. Others are in Grade 12, standing on the verge of transition from the known to the new. Some have been in the work world, for a year or many, and are nurturing a vision of growth and change. Others are raising your own families. For some of you, Canada will be a brand new adventure.

Whatever your starting point, if you are uncertain about how to begin your preparation for post-secondary education and a career, you are certainly not alone. We've worked with hundreds of students, all of whom have asked (and answered) the questions you'll find addressed here. They learned through seeking experience, making mistakes, doing things the hard way, progressing a little at a time. We hope their experience, and ours, will help make your planning for — and life at — college easier, fuller, less stressful and more rewarding.

We share many real life stories in these pages. We've added tips and hints for your ready reference. Checklists, questionnaires, and worksheets invite your participation. Crack this book wide open! Get out your most colourful pens and make it yours!

(A brief note about style: our guess is that about half of you are women, and half are men. For ease of reading, we use *he* or *she* interchangeably. Anywhere we use *he, she* applies equally well, and vice versa.)

Our aim is to provide you with a tool-kit. Open it when you have need of a tool. Use it to find information, develop a skill, solve a problem, or remind yourself that you are OK. This is not a book to read from cover to cover, unless you are the sort of person who does this with books. Rather, it is a resource to dip into and use when you need to. We hope *College Smarts™* will become your companion, providing you with the guidelines and support you need to make competent, strategic, informed choices about your education and your career.

Introduction to Our Readers' Parents

Hints

The Parent's Guide Home Page (started by Peter Cowley, a parent in British Columbia) can be a good resource. It includes a question and answer section, as well as opportunities for discussion. It's at www.parentsguide.com

Welcome to the Brave New World of student life and parenting! We're sure you've noticed — probably with trepidation — that times have changed since your generation was at college. Today, becoming a post-secondary student is a serious business, undertaken amid job uncertainties, funding crunches, vigorous competition, strong pressure for grades, and rapid technological change. Choice is everywhere. University is neither the only nor the best educational alternative for every eager student. New institutional options abound, each with their own advantages, disadvantages, and possibility for your child's future.

Many of you feel the same confusion that your children experience, with the added pressure of believing you must have all the answers (should they happen to ask). This book is, therefore, written for your students *and for you*. As seasoned psychologists, career planners, and educators we've counselled, taught, and coached several thousand students and their parents. We've also offered support and guidance to our own seven children, as they navigated the maze of occupational and educational alternatives.

As parents, we discovered (tripped over) many roadblocks when it came to advising our children. Often, emotion ran high and objectivity low. Our children seemed reluctant to take parental suggestions seriously! Yet researchers assure us that most students need and value their parents' wisdom. How, then, do we best proceed?

Consultants

Our tips for parents are addressed "To the Consultant."

Our work taught us one simple principle: students thrive when parents treat them as equals. We will coach you to relinquish your typical parental role and learn a new perspective: the role of the **consultant**. Your student becomes your valued **client**. On this new footing, creative and fruitful discussion can occur.

Treat this book as your consultant's manual, in the same way that it is your client's handbook. We invite you to shift to a position of equality in your parent/child relationship (and help your client to do the same). Listen more, talk less, and engage your client in a dialogue. We hope *College Smarts*™ will answer some of the hundreds of questions you and your clients are asking. Our wish for your clients is probably the same as yours: a rewarding, meaningful post-secondary education which carries them in the direction of their dreams.

*part
one:*

Get
Ready:
Start
Smart

1

Whether you are a Grade 11 student beginning to consider your options, a twenty-something employee who is ready to go back to school, or a thirty-something parent embarking on part-time studies, the best place to start your education is to think about who you are. The more you know about yourself, the more power you have to make good decisions about your education. We invite you to begin your educational journey by climbing the self-assessment pyramid — at the top is a terrific career choice which is perfectly suited to you!

The following pages are full of activities for you to do: checklists, questionnaires, reviews, thinking opportunities. Each of these activities is intended to guide you, step-by-step, up the pyramid. Each is based on years of research about what makes good educational choices possible. Each will bring you closer to your goal. It doesn't matter whether your goal is a highly-focused education aimed at a specific career, or a broad, general education aimed at furthering your knowledge base. Either way, you'll be faced with an incredible number of choices, first about what school you will attend, and then about what program of study you will follow once you get there. The self-assessment pyramid builds the base from which you can make those choices effectively.

Let's begin . . .

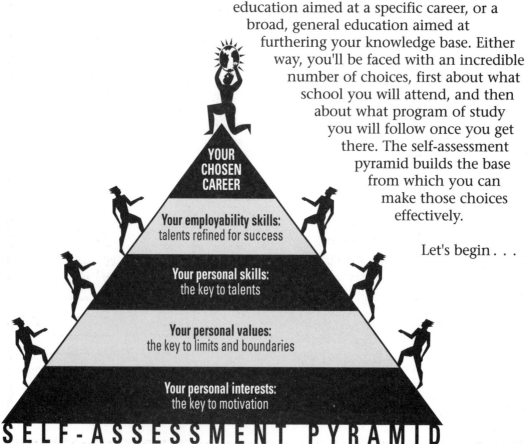

YOUR CHOSEN CAREER

Your employability skills: talents refined for success

Your personal skills: the key to talents

Your personal values: the key to limits and boundaries

Your personal interests: the key to motivation

SELF-ASSESSMENT PYRAMID

1. What are your interests?

Hints

Make the checklists and other activities in this book fun for you!

This is an examination of your personality! Express yourself! Create your own colour system — red-hot colours for things that really excite you; cool-blue colours for those that put you to sleep. Or design a symbols system — what symbol could you use to identify those items which have real appeal?

Knowing yourself begins with knowing your interests. We start here because your interests are the strongest predictor of your career success. This is good common sense, if you think about it. Inevitably, interests are the key to motivation. If you are interested in something, you are certainly more inclined to spend your energy (and your time, and your money) becoming good at that something. It's human nature.

The Interests Checklist below will prompt you to think about a wide range of activities, or types of activities. What excites you? What makes you look forward to getting out of bed in the morning? What makes life worthwhile? Don't worry yet about whether you could ever find a job that includes such activities. That comes later. Just go through the checklist, follow the directions, and learn something about yourself.

INTERESTS CHECKLIST

Check off the activities that you enjoy (or think you would enjoy). Add any that are not listed here.

•

Place 2 check marks next to those you would like to include as part of your work.

•

Circle the top 5, to identify them clearly

•

Draw a line through those that have no appeal for you.

- ☐ Acting
- ☐ Being expressive
- ☐ Being imaginative
- ☐ Being sociable
- ☐ Caring for children
- ☐ Collecting things
- ☐ Computers
- ☐ Crafts
- ☐ Cooking
- ☐ Creating artistic things
- ☐ Dancing
- ☐ Debating
- ☐ Decorating
- ☐ Designing
- ☐ Drawing/painting
- ☐ Entertaining
- ☐ Exercising
- ☐ Fixing and repairing
- ☐ Helping people
- ☐ Helping society
- ☐ Improving environment

- ☐ Inventing
- ☐ Learning/ understanding
- ☐ Listening
- ☐ Making money
- ☐ Making things with my hands
- ☐ Mathematics/ working with numbers
- ☐ Music
- ☐ Observing & collecting data
- ☐ Organizing & directing activities
- ☐ Organizing & directing people
- ☐ Outdoor activities
- ☐ Persuading
- ☐ Public speaking
- ☐ Reading
- ☐ Religion
- ☐ Researching

- ☐ Science experiments
- ☐ Solving problems
- ☐ Sports
- ☐ Starting a project
- ☐ Teaching
- ☐ Acting
- ☐ Travelling
- ☐ Using office equipment
- ☐ Using tools & machinery
- ☐ Volunteering
- ☐ Working with animals
- ☐ Working with money
- ☐ _____
- ☐ _____
- ☐ _____
- ☐ _____
- ☐ _____
- ☐ _____
- ☐ _____

If you have completed all the steps on the Interests Checklist, you will now have at least five circled activities that have real appeal for you. Take those Top Five interests and rewrite them into the "Fabulous Interests I Can't Ignore" summary table below. Now, you have an opportunity to think up some strategies for pursuing these interests. Do your interests influence how you spend your time each day? Do they determine what you choose to read? Are they a part of your friendships? Is there a volunteer opportunity out there with your name on it? What do you want to learn more about?

FABULOUS INTERESTS I CAN'T IGNORE

MY TOP 5 INTERESTS	MY STRATEGIES FOR PURSUING
Example: Organizing People	Organize class reunion, river clean-up, food bank drive.
1.	
2.	
3.	
4.	
5.	

2. Next, consider your personal values...

Personal values are another way of looking at what is most important. Values describe our deeply-held beliefs about what really matters. Your values are your own, and yet they will have been influenced by your family, the way you were raised, your culture, the people you hang out with, your education and your personal experience.

Human beings hold many values in common. It is not unusual to look at the checklist below and think, "All of these values are important to me." The real test is in beginning to sort out what is most important. Knowing what's most important creates limits and boundaries in your search for the right career. If a particular career option is not congruent with your most important values, it is probably not a good choice for you. So give some consideration to the ranking of your values, using the "What's really and truly most important" summary table which follows. This is an important step on the journey up the self-assessment pyramid.

VALUES CHECKLIST

- ☐ Being an expert
- ☐ Belonging to groups
- ☐ Competition
- ☐ Creativity
- ☐ Decision making
- ☐ Excitement
- ☐ Freedom
- ☐ Friendship
- ☐ Helping others
- ☐ Helping society
- ☐ Independence
- ☐ Money
- ☐ People contact
- ☐ Power
- ☐ Precise work
- ☐ Recognition
- ☐ Responsibility
- ☐ Security
- ☐ Stability
- ☐ Status
- ☐ Stimulation
- ☐ Travelling
- ☐ Variety
- ☐ Working Alone
- ☐ _____
- ☐ _____
- ☐ _____

WHAT'S REALLY AND TRULY MOST IMPORTANT

RANK	VALUE
1.	
2.	
3.	
4.	
5.	

Hints

As you go through the values checklist below, you will notice some items which sound similar to the interests checklist you have just completed. That is intentional. Remember, interests describe what you like to do. Values describe what you care about deeply.

Consultants

Have you talked about what is most important in your own work?

Job satisfaction? Money? Accomplishment?

Complete the values checklist for yourself, and then talk about it with your client. Our bet is you'll get to know something new about each other!

Michael was a good student in high school who (encouraged by his school counsellor and his parents) enrolled in Engineering. After failing his first year, he moved to a different university – and again enrolled in Engineering. His father stressed the importance of a good, solid professional degree, and encouraged Michael to pursue the field despite his early failures. But Michael failed again. He was badly demoralized and wondered if he was stupid. Fortunately, focused career planning with an industrial psychologist helped him recognize his excitement for and interest in Business and Commerce. He knew he had a natural bent for business – which career planning helped him confirm. He enrolled in a Commerce program, and graduated with academic success and a clear career goal.

12 HOT TRANSFERABLE SKILLS

•

Check off the skills you are good at and the ones you need work on

•

Notice how many of these skills can be acquired outside the workplace, as well as in it.

- ☐ Computer literacy
- ☐ Budget or money management
- ☐ Time management/ coping with deadline pressure
- ☐ Communicating clearly orally and in writing
- ☐ Listening
- ☐ Organizing/managing/ co-ordinating
- ☐ Problem solving
- ☐ Openness to new ideas and ways of doing things
- ☐ Negotiating/arbitration
- ☐ Team playing
- ☐ Ability to work with numbers
- ☐ Knowing how to learn

3 What are your talents and skills?
(and what do you want them to be?)

Now, as you continue up the self-assessment pyramid, it is time to think about your talents, your abilities, your skills. What are you good at now? What do you want to be good at over time? Where do your talents lie? The skills you develop, through your experience and through your education, are your passport to success. Remember as you work at this section — skills can be learned. In the following exercises there will be some skills you already have, and some you want to master.

There are many different ways of thinking about and categorizing skills. There are **technical skills** — those which evolve from specific knowledge and require specific training. There are **self-management skills** — those which reflect personal attitudes and attributes such as dependability, punctuality, tolerance, enthusiasm, persistence, self-control, goal-orientation, cooperation.

Some of the most important skills today are **trans-ferable skills** — those which you can use, and which are essential to your success, in many different work settings. These include such critical abilities as literacy, numeracy, computer literacy, oral and written commun-ication, and the ability to access information. This means you need to be able to read, spell and write accurately, as well as express your thoughts effectively; problem-solve; work with numbers; and use a variety of software programs. As you can see, human beings can be skilled in many, many different ways.

Begin to think about your skill set by completing the Skills Checklist on the following pages. There are a great variety of skills listed here. The checklist will give you an opportunity to remind yourself of the skills you already have, and to think about those you would like to develop.

Look over the Skills Checklist and mark off those skills you have observed in your client (use a different coloured marker). Give some examples of how and when you have seen these skills in action. This may encourage further discussion, build confidence, and open up additional career options.

SKILLS CHECKLIST

The following checklist gives you an opportunity to remind yourself of the skills you have, as well as those you would like to develop.

Check (✓) the skills you have now
Double-check (✓✓) the skills you want to develop
Think about occupations in which you might be able to use some or many of these skills.

COMMUNICATION SKILLS

- [ ] Editing
- [ ] Explaining
- [ ] Interviewing
- [ ] Listening
- [ ] Negotiating
- [ ] Persuading
- [ ] Public Speaking
- [ ] Questioning
- [ ] Reading
- [ ] Spelling
- [ ] Talking
- [ ] Writing

CREATIVE SKILLS

- [ ] Creating/inventing
- [ ] Designing/displaying
- [ ] Drawing/painting/ sculpting
- [ ] Improvising/adapting/ experimenting
- [ ] Perceiving intuitively
- [ ] Performing/entertaining
- [ ] Visualizing/ imagining
- [ ] Writing/playwriting/ composing

DETAIL SKILLS

- [ ] Alertness
- [ ] Attention to detail
- [ ] Being precise
- [ ] Using caution
- [ ] Following procedures
- [ ] Record keeping
- [ ] Sorting
- [ ] Verifying

LEADERSHIP SKILLS

- [ ] Administering
- [ ] Confronting
- [ ] Delegating
- [ ] Directing/supervising
- [ ] Initiating
- [ ] Making decisions
- [ ] Organizing
- [ ] Planning

PERSONAL SKILLS

- [ ] Conformity
- [ ] Dependability
- [ ] Drive
- [ ] Efficiency
- [ ] Enthusiasm
- [ ] Flexibility
- [ ] Integrity
- [ ] Loyalty
- [ ] Persistence
- [ ] Positive attitude
- [ ] Pride in performance
- [ ] Punctuality
- [ ] Tact
- [ ] Understanding

PHYSICAL SKILLS

- [ ] Acting quickly
- [ ] Manual dexterity
- [ ] Motor co-ordination
- [ ] Stamina
- [ ] Strength

REASONING SKILLS

- [ ] Analyzing
- [ ] Investigating/ researching
- [ ] Remembering
- [ ] Synthesizing

SENSORY SKILLS

- [ ] Sound discrimination
- [ ] Colour discrimination
- [ ] Shape discrimination
- [ ] Depth discrimination

A

SKILLS CHECKLIST...cont'd

WORKING-WITH-DIFFICULT-SITUATION SKILLS

- ☐ Dealing with emergencies
- ☐ Performing repetitive tasks
- ☐ Responding to feedback
- ☐ Risk taking
- ☐ Self control
- ☐ Tolerating discomfort
- ☐ Working under pressure

WORKING-WITH-TOOLS OR MACHINES SKILLS

- ☐ Adjusting
- ☐ Assembling
- ☐ Building/ constructing
- ☐ Fixing/repairing
- ☐ Installing
- ☐ Mechanical reasoning
- ☐ Operating

WORKING-WITH-NUMBERS SKILLS

- ☐ Budgeting
- ☐ Calculating

- ☐ Counting
- ☐ Estimating
- ☐ Measuring
- ☐ Numerical Reasoning

WORKING-WITH-OTHERS SKILLS

- ☐ Advising/counselling
- ☐ Co-operating
- ☐ Protecting/guarding
- ☐ Serving
- ☐ Teaching/ training
- ☐ Treating

As you have done at previous levels, work with the skills checklist now to build your Top Five Incredible Skills Summary. Start with your top 5 skill categories (include those which you have now and those which you want to develop). Make a note of specific skills within those categories. Then think about some potential careers in which you might be able to use these skills.

MY TOP FIVE INCREDIBLE SKILLS SUMMARY

TOP 5 SKILL CATEGORIES	SPECIFIC SKILLS	POTENTIAL CAREERS
Example: *Leadership*	*Organizing, planning, delegating*	*Manager, teacher*
1.		
2.		
3.		
4.		
5.		

4: Assessing your skills, continued - considering employability

Another way to examine your skills, in preparation for pursuing your education, is to think in terms of employability skills. **Employability skills are critical.** They are those fundamental skills, attitudes and behaviours that any employer looks for.

What are the skills employers consider essential and fundamental? The Corporate Council on Education conducted a study in which researchers found that employers are looking for people with three sets of critical attributes: *Academic Skills, Personal Management Skills, and Teamwork Skills.*

ACADEMIC SKILLS are absolutely essential to get, keep and progress on a job — and to achieve the best results for you and your employer. Employers define academic skills as the ability to *communicate, think and learn.*

You demonstrate the ability to *communicate* if you can: understand and speak the languages in which business is conducted; listen and respond effectively; read, comprehend and use written materials, including graphs, charts and displays; and write well in the languages in which business is done.

You will also be required to *think* critically and act logically to evaluate situations, solve problems and make decisions. You will be called upon to understand and solve problems involving mathematics; to use technology, instruments, and information systems effectively; and to access and apply specialized knowledge from various fields (e.g. skilled trades, technology, physical sciences, arts and social sciences).

Without a doubt, in today's world, you will be expected to continue to *learn* for the rest of your working life.

Personal Management Skills include those attitudes and behaviours which are as fundamental and significant as the academic skills outlined above — if your goal is to get, keep and progress on a job, and to achieve the best results. Employers seek out people who can demonstrate: *positive attitudes, responsibility, and adaptability.* The necessary *positive attitudes* include: self-esteem and confidence; honesty, integrity and personal ethics; a willingness to learn, grow and stay healthy; and initiative, energy and persistence to get the job done.

If you act with *responsibility,* you will be able to set goals and priorities in both work and personal life; plan and manage time, money and other resources to achieve your goals; and be accountable for the actions you have taken.

You will show *adaptability* if you demonstrate a positive attitude toward change; recognition of and respect for diversity and individual difference; and the creativity to identify and suggest new ideas to get the job done.

Teamwork Skills are fundamental to working with others on a job — and working with others makes achieving the best results possible. Employers are looking for people who can *work effectively in community.* This includes the ability to understand and contribute to the organization's goals; to be aware of the team's culture; to make joint decisions; to respect differing opinions; to exercise "give and take" in pursuit of group results; to adopt a team approach when appropriate and to lead when necessary.

In addition to these three employability skill sets, we would add one more which we consider critical to success in the working world — entrepreneurial skills.

ENTREPRENEURIAL SKILLS are those skills that evolve from thinking of yourself as a business: ME Inc. Whether you choose to work for yourself as a self-employed entrepreneur, or to work for someone else as an other-employed entrepreneur, the skills you use to *market yourself* are becoming ever more important. Dorothy Leeds, who wrote a book called *Marketing Yourself,* suggests that the most successful workers of the future will be those who apply marketing principles to their careers. "Career entrepreneurs" are identified by the following ten skills or mindsets:

- **Adaptability:** change is an opportunity, not an obstacle.
- **Decisiveness:** making choices and decisions, and learning from mistakes.
- **Planning ahead:** being future-oriented.
- **Commitment:** to service and to the customer.
- **Communication:** saying what you mean, and being understood.
- **Self-evaluation:** asking yourself what improvements you can make.
- **Creativity:** finding ways for you and your customers to win.
- **Independence:** relying on your own abilities for results.
- **Cooperation:** being a team player.
- **Adding value:** giving more than was promised or expected.

To learn more about becoming an entrepreneur, join a Junior Achievement group, or talk to your local Chamber of Commerce about setting up a program at your school.

Many students develop entrepreneurial skills by running their own businesses while still in school. Typical examples include: a paper route, snow-blowing contract, lawn care and pruning services, house-sitting, database inputting and updates, software programming, running a computer help desk. Managing your own small business gives you the opportunity to make money; learn to manage finances, people, and budgets; become a skilled marketer; develop a strong work ethic; and provide excellent service. These skills will certainly enhance your resume. Employers always look for self-starters.

Now, climb to the top of the self-assessment pyramid by thinking about your skills specifically in terms of employability. The following checklist invites you to rate your employability skills as strong/ moderate/ needs improvement.

In this exercise, we also challenge you to identify "how do you know?" Do you know you have "strong" listening skills because your friends often tell you so? Do you know you have a "needs improvement" sense of responsibility because you often miss commitments or deadlines? Do you know you have a "strong" creativity skill set because you are constantly overflowing with new ideas? Thinking about the evidence of your skills will help you get honest, and get specific, about what you naturally bring to the workplace and what you need to work on.

We include two copies of the Employability Skills Checklist because this is a good time to ask someone who knows you well for feedback. It is not unusual for other people to see our skills more clearly than we can see them ourselves. Give the second checklist to a trusted teacher, employer, parent, or honest friend, and ask that person to help you identify your strengths and weaknesses in this critical area of skill development. Asking for direct feedback takes some courage — but if you ask the right person, the results will be invaluable!

EMPLOYABILITY SKILLS CHECKLIST

SELF-ASSESSMENT	STRONG	MOD	IMPROVE	HOW DO YOU KNOW?
Academic Skills:				
Communication:				
Listening				
Understanding				
Reading				
Writing				
Spelling				
Grammar				
Thinking:				
Evaluate information				
Solve problems				
Make decisions				
Plan ahead				
Work with numbers				
Technical Skills:				
Computer literate				
Personal Management Skills:				
Positive attitudes				
Positive behaviours				
Responsible				
Adaptable				
Creative				
Teamwork Skills:				
Work with others				
Contribute to goals				
Plan & make joint decisions				

EMPLOYABILITY SKILLS CHECKLIST

SELF-ASSESSMENT	STRONG	MOD	IMPROVE	HOW DO YOU KNOW?
Support outcomes				
Respect others				
Give and take				
Marketing/				
Entrepreneurial Skills:				
Decisiveness				
Self-evaluation				
Independence				
Co-operation				
Persistence				
Creativity (ideas)				
Friendly				
Accountability:				
Keep my word				
Follow through				
Do my best				
Responsible for my actions				
Other Important Skills:				

EMPLOYABILITY SKILLS CHECKLIST

OTHER'S ASSESSMENT	STRONG	MOD	IMPROVE	HOW DO YOU KNOW?
Academic Skills:				
Communication:				
Listening				
Understanding				
Reading				
Writing				
Spelling				
Grammar				
Thinking:				
Evaluate information				
Solve problems				
Make decisions				
Plan ahead				
Work with numbers				
Technical Skills:				
Computer literate				
Personal Management				
Skills:				
Positive attitudes				
Positive behaviours				
Responsible				
Adaptable				
Creative				
Teamwork Skills:				
Work with others				
Contribute to goals				
Plan & make joint decisions				

EMPLOYABILITY SKILLS CHECKLIST

OTHER'S ASSESSMENT	STRONG	MOD	IMPROVE	HOW DO YOU KNOW?
Support outcomes				
Respect others				
Give and take				
Marketing/				
Entrepreneurial Skills:				
Decisiveness				
Self-evaluation				
Independence				
Co-operation				
Persistence				
Creativity (ideas)				
Friendly				
Accountability:				
Keep my word				
Follow through				
Do my best				
Responsible for my actions				
Other Important Skills:				

Complete this process by writing your employability skills in the "Employers Will Love Me" summary table below. First, note your top five employability skills. Second, note the five employability skills that you most need to develop (these are the skills which you know will be important to you, and which you rated as "needs improvement" in your checklist). Third, jot down some ideas about how you will develop those skills that you most need to improve.

EMPLOYERS WILL LOVE ME

TOP 5 SKILLS	5 'NEEDS IMPROVEMENT' SKILLS	STRATEGIES FOR IMPROVEMENT
1.	1.	
2.	2.	
3.	3.	
4.	4.	
5.	5.	

CONGRATULATIONS!!! YOU ARE AWESOME!!!
You have now climbed the self-assessment pyramid. With a bird's eye view from the top, you have vastly improved your chances of spotting the educational opportunities and career choices that are right for you. You have also set in motion an important, ongoing process — the process of making decisions and choices in your life based on what is true for you. There are lots more choices to make on this journey. Carry on!

Start with an attitude adjustment...

No matter what the state of the economy at any given time, know that you are an individual with many abilities and interests — some of which will translate into work that you will find challenging and satisfying. The way you do this work may be different than you expect, or than it was for your parents. Traditional working styles and expectations (eight-hour work days, permanent employment, predictable schedules, automatic vacation and benefits) are increasingly being replaced by contract work, staggered hours, fluctuating income, self-managed careers, and an "attitude of entrepreneurism." Dream about doing work you enjoy, and develop the talents and skills necessary to do the work that appeals to you.

The need for an attitude of entrepreneurism does not translate into less available work, or fewer options for the next generation, or anything of the sort. It does mean some redefining of work — and some reconsideration of our expectations. Successful work experiences are almost always available. You do need to prepare for them, however. Preparation will mean training, education, and continuous learning over a lifetime.

Hints

The five statements highlighted here form the basis for a very important attitude adjustment. Copy these statements down somewhere you will see them regularly — in your calendar, on a post-it note which you stick on your mirror, or on a card for your wallet. Think about what these statements mean for you. The result will be a high level of independence, and accountability.

**Attitude of Entrepreneurism = Me Inc.
I am my own Career Manager.
Employees = Service/product providers.
Employers = clients.
The world is my Market Place.**

Then learn more about where the jobs are...

Think about what industries are attractive to you. Companies come and go, and occupations change. But if your industry is growing, you will always find work — especially if you are open to growth and are willing to retrain, upgrade, and learn continuously. In order to select your target industries, research and read up on:

- Which industry and service sectors are expected to survive and thrive?
- Where, in the world, will those industries operate?
- How will businesses (and you) need to adapt, in order to stay competitive?
- Where are the well-positioned companies and how can you recognize them?
- What specific skills, personal characteristics, and education will you need to develop a career, market yourself successfully, and stay current and competitive?

There are innumerable sources of information on employment opportunities. The business section of the local newspaper, national media of all kinds, your community Chamber of Commerce, current government publications, and any number of books on career planning are good places to start. Or simply talk to people — the optician who fits your glasses, your dentist, a cab driver, the plumber who is replacing your kitchen taps. Try to visit work places to get an inside look. Ask your parents to talk about what they do; do the same with relatives and your friends' parents (or your parents' friends).

Two of our favourite Canadian books on the subject of employment are:

Nuala Beck
Excelerate: Growing in the New Economy
Toronto: HarperCollins, 1995

and

Colin Campbell
Where The Jobs Are: Career Survival For Canadians In The New Global Economy
Toronto: McFarlane, Walter & Ross, 1997.

Consider some strong career prospects...

Over the next ten years, as always, some industries will grow, others will remain fairly static, and still others will be on the decline or fading into the sunset (as in the term "sunset industries"). Some industries have been dormant, but are now in a comeback mode. Often, traditional career paths in an industry are closing even as new, creative paths are opening up to those who can spot them.

Nuala Beck, in her book *Excelerate* (1995), ranks industries in the same way that the hotel and tourist trade ranks hotels and restaurants (note the sample categories as adapted on the next page). Her "five-star industries" are worth considering. They are fast-growing opportunities with strong career prospects. These industries offer continued job creation, maximum job security (if such a concept still has relevance), good to excellent salaries (for the most part), and most importantly, a growing knowledge base.

TECHNOLOGICAL

Agriculture Chemicals and Fertilizer Manufacturing
Communications/Telecommunications
Electrical and Electronic Equipment Wholesalers
Engineering, Design, Technical and Scientific Services
Natural Gas Distribution Systems
Pharmaceutical Manufacturing
Pipeline Transportation
Plastics and Synthetic Resins Manufacturing
Software and Computer Services
Waste Management/Environmental Protection

HEALTH CARE/EDUCATION/SOCIAL SERVICES

Health Practitioners In Independent Practice:
    Chiropractors, Dentists, Doctors, Nurses,
    Optometrists, Physical Therapists, Speech-language
    Pathologists, and their support staff (professional
    salaries good, support staff salaries low)
Hospitals (moderate salaries for non-professional staff)
Elementary and Secondary Schools
Universities (moderate salaries)
Recreational Sports and Clubs (very low salaries)
Community-based Social Services (low salaries)

BUSINESS/FINANCE

Accounting Firms and Bookkeeping for Entrepreneurs
(moderate salaries)
Consumer and Business Financing
Investment Management (for those professionals who
adapt to the changing marketplace)
Motion Picture, Video and Sound Recording
Newspaper and Magazine Publishing and Printing

Be Smart and Wary!
Professions and Industries in Transition...

Most professions and industries are experiencing an incredible pace of change. The traditional approach to a career in many industries is on the wane. This creates more opportunities — and more need — to be creative. Here is a brief sampling of the kinds of change you will experience in the marketplace, and some suggestions about how to make that change work for you. As you conduct your research in various industries, watch carefully for the new, innovative, creative opportunities that are opening.

Lawyers — The traditional market is fairly saturated. Fields of specialization are changing. Clients are becoming more sophisticated and knowledgeable. Choose fields like environmental law, intellectual property law, health law, biomedical ethics, human rights law, native law, international law, and advocacy.

Librarians — Many former and current library users are increasingly accessing the Internet for their information. The "smart" libraries will become virtual libraries and information distributors, providing immediate access around the world.

Advertising Agencies — The successful will adapt aggressively to the new advertising media. There are some growing opportunities — the Internet, consulting with clients who use their own desktop publishing capabilities, advising on new technology, and (as always in this business!) being quicker, smarter and more original than your competitors.

If you need further help (as many people do), we encourage you to do some more in-depth career planning, either by consulting a psychologist specializing in career planning, or by using our companion workbook, Career Smarts™ (publication information available at the back of this volume).

Pharmacies — Although the demand for prescription drugs is rising, people will make fewer trips to the pharmacy. Increasingly, buyers are likely to use 1-800 ordering, or go to the "Big Box" drug superstores in search of discounts. Smart career seekers in this field will focus on research and development in pharmaceutical companies, emphasize consumer education, and partner with health care providers to promote wellness.

Publishers — The potential exists to succeed, for those who shift gears and adapt to the new economy. The best will be small, independent and creative. Publishing services will be tied to marketing strategies, CD-Roms will be a major product opportunity, and a high-tech knowledge base will be necessary to adapt to new opportunities.

Broadcasting — More and more broadcasting functions are "canned" or pre-recorded. Look for options in pre-recording programs, and develop your skills in public relations, as well as theatre, film and video production.

- *How much does your client know about your work?*
- *Have you changed jobs/careers? Does your client know why?*
- *Do you discuss work at home with your client?*
- *How much do you enjoy your work?*
- *If you could choose, what would you choose to do now, and in the future?*
- *How do you feel about the probability of multiple career changes for your client?*

Spend time on the following activities:
- *Ask your client to describe in detail her "perfect career."*
- *Invite her to come to your place of work and observe, participate, ask questions.*
- *Arrange with her to observe others at work and discuss her observations.*
- *Encourage her to look ahead twenty years and imagine what her work will be like.*
- *Talk about what you both feel is important about work. Is it job satisfaction? Money? Accomplishment?*

Finally, the Career Sampler

Now is the ideal time for another checklist! Following is a sampling of careers that might interest you. Consider the options and check off those that have a strong appeal. Or start by crossing off those that have no appeal whatsoever, and work backwards! Go back to your other checklists and consider your interests, values, and skills. Where are the good fits?

CAREER SAMPLER

BUSINESS

- [ ] Advertising account executive
- [ ] Bookkeeper
- [ ] Buyer/purchasing officer
- [ ] Clerk (accounting, admitting, car rental, library, payroll)
- [ ] Computer operator
- [ ] Fund raiser
- [ ] Human resources specialist
- [ ] Land developer
- [ ] Marketing specialist
- [ ] Medical transcriptionist
- [ ] Production co-ordinator
- [ ] Property manager
- [ ] Publisher
- [ ] Receptionist
- [ ] Secretary
- [ ] Stockbroker
- [ ] Travel consultant
- [ ] Word processor operator

FINE ARTS

Art/Music

- [ ] Architect
- [ ] Artist
- [ ] Cartoonist
- [ ] Crafts person
- [ ] Conservation & restoration technician
- [ ] Designer (costume, floral, graphic, packaging etc.)
- [ ] Engraver
- [ ] Illustrator
- [ ] Musician/music teacher
- [ ] Special effects technician
- [ ] Therapist (art, music)
- [ ] Window dresser

Drama

- [ ] Actor
- [ ] Camera operator
- [ ] Film/video editor
- [ ] Make-up artist
- [ ] Playwright
- [ ] Production assistant
- [ ] Stage manager
- [ ] Stunt performer
- [ ] Talent scout
- [ ] Wardrobe supervisor

HOME ECONOMICS

- [ ] Clothing & textiles buyer
- [ ] Costume restorer
- [ ] Dietitian
- [ ] Interior designer
- [ ] Product developer/tester/promoter
- [ ] Residential realtor

INDUSTRIAL

Construction & Fabrication

- [ ] Boilermaker
- [ ] Building construction inspector
- [ ] Cabinetmaker
- [ ] Cost estimator
- [ ] Furnace installer/repairer
- [ ] Gemologist
- [ ] Lens grinder
- [ ] Locksmith
- [ ] Machinist
- [ ] Sporting goods repairer

Electricity/Electronics

- [ ] Aircraft instrument mechanic
- [ ] Explosives handler
- [ ] Fibre-optics specialist
- [ ] Power lineperson
- [ ] Radio operator (drilling rig, air, marine)
- [ ] Technician (biomedical, broadcast electronics, radio/sonar etc.)

Mechanics

- [ ] Airport maintenance worker
- [ ] Appliance servicer
- [ ] Mechanic (auto body, motor, refrigeration)
- [ ] Operator (ski lift, heavy equipment, oil and gas equipment)
- [ ] Utility worker (power, gas, telephone)

Graphic Communications

- [ ] Architectural technician
- [ ] Cartographer
- [ ] Computer-assisted graphics
- [ ] Layout artist
- [ ] Drafter
- [ ] Photographic process worker
- [ ] Printing and graphic arts craftperson (bindary worker, typesetter)
- [ ] Silkscreener

LANGUAGE ARTS

- [ ] Air traffic controller
- [ ] Announcer/commentator
- [ ] Cataloguer
- [ ] Editor (book, magazine, newspaper, film, TV)
- [ ] Educator
- [ ] Journalist
- [ ] Librarian
- [ ] Public relations specialist

☐ Salesperson (insurance, radio/TV, retail, real estate)

MATHEMATICS

☐ Accountant
☐ Actuary
☐ Artificial intelligence expert
☐ Claims adjuster
☐ Corporate planner
☐ Grain elevator agent
☐ Insurance underwriter
☐ Statistician
☐ Systems analyst

PHYSICAL EDUCATION

☐ Athlete
☐ Camp counsellor
☐ Coach
☐ Fitness consultant
☐ Golf/tennis pro
☐ Guide (fishing, hunting, mountain)
☐ Lifeguard
☐ Recreation specialist (prison, theme park, disabilities)
☐ Ski patroller

SCIENCE

☐ Agriculturist
☐ Airline pilot
☐ Apiarist/beekeeper
☐ Arborist/tree surgeon
☐ Audiology technician
☐ Blood clinic assistant
☐ Chemist (criminological, clinical, environmental, quality control)
☐ Chiropractor

☐ Curator, zoo
☐ Dentist
☐ Denturist
☐ Dental assistant
☐ Engineer
☐ Florist
☐ Geologist
☐ Geophysicist
☐ Geneticist
☐ Greenhouse operator
☐ Hazardous waste management specialist
☐ Laboratory technician
☐ Nurse
☐ Occupational therapist
☐ Oil field service operator
☐ Oncologist
☐ Park ranger
☐ Pharmacist
☐ Physician/surgeon
☐ Physical therapist
☐ Prospector
☐ Respiratory therapist
☐ Seismologist
☐ Speech language pathologist
☐ Software developer
☐ Taxidermist
☐ Technician (engineering, air conditioning, fish and wildlife, garbage disposal, medical equipment)
☐ Tree planter

SECOND LANGUAGES

☐ Diplomat
☐ Flight attendant
☐ Immigration aide worker
☐ Interpreter
☐ Travel guide/tour escort

SOCIAL STUDIES & SOCIAL SCIENCES

☐ Analyst (jobs/occupations, labour force, opinion, etc.)
☐ Archeologist
☐ Community development officer/social planner
☐ Counsellor (career, educational, employment, leisure, marriage)
☐ Criminologist
☐ Dealer (antiques, art, stamp)
☐ Economist
☐ Foreign service officer/diplomat
☐ Geographer
☐ Lawyer
☐ Politician
☐ Psychologist
☐ Religious education worker
☐ Staff trainer/Human Resource specialist
☐ Teacher
☐ Volunteer co-ordinator

Now, once again, summarize what you have learned from working through the checklist. Enter your top five career choices (at this point) in the "Five Careers that Might Make Me Happy" summary table below. Then think about ways you could conduct additional research into these options. List your research strategies. Who could you talk to? What could you read? Where could you search for information?

5 CAREERS THAT MIGHT MAKE ME HAPPY	
CAREERS	**RESEARCH**
Example: **Architect**	*Talk to architects, read, look at design books, visit university programs.*
1.	
2.	
3.	
4.	
5.	

A

We asked all kinds of university students, "What is the single most useful piece of advice you could give to high school students who are planning to attend college or university?" Their answers...

Plan ahead.
Start early in Grade 10.
Get good grades.
Keep your options open.
Learn word processing.

Much of this wisdom comes from hindsight. We offer it to you so that you can benefit from their lessons, learned through experience and sometimes the hard way!

Six Brilliant Things to do While You're in Grade Ten

Grade 10 is a great time to begin your planning. Your "window of opportunity" is wide open right now. That window will get smaller as you progress through to Grade 12. Build on your current advantage!

1. Choose academic courses, and keep your options open. Be sure to include Math — and plan to complete all the Algebra, Geometry and Trigonometry requirements, even if they sound a bit daunting at the moment. The leap to high school math is a smart challenge to take on. Add Calculus if you might want to study Engineering, Computer Science, or Technology later. Almost every university now requires Math as an admission pre-requisite. Seriously consider taking sciences — biology, physics and chemistry — even if you plan to pursue studies in the Fine Arts, Social Sciences or Humanities. There are very few programs where the sciences are not needed, at least in some form. Instead of taking a spare, fill that time with a science or language (it is possible to save socializing for the weekend!).

2. Develop good study skills. Use the Study Skills section in this book — it will give you a great head start. Practice the strategies we suggest. Modify them to suit your style. Get into the habit of "smart" studying early

If you participate in athletics, be careful not to sacrifice academics. Even if you plan to be an athlete, you will need good grades to win athletic scholarships, or to be accepted into an athletic program. Don't put all your eggs in one basket!

— you will save yourself hundreds of hours over the next few years and maybe even have time for fun!

3. Polish your language and communication skills. Read, write, debate, act, speak in public. This is invaluable practice for making presentations, writing assignments and doing projects at high school and university — and for bringing great transferable skills to the work world later on.

4. Build your word processing skills. Learn a word processing program and use it for writing your essays and assignments. This skill is essential in college or university. Many schools no longer accept handwritten assignments — too many students have terrible handwriting, and instructors don't have time to figure out the scribbles. What's more, good keyboarding skills will save you another several hundred hours over your university career. After that, a typical career person may spend a minimum of 2 hours a day using a word processor; over a working life of 40 years, that's more than 17,000 hours!

Practice thinking directly onto your keyboard, instead of writing everything first in longhand. Thinking and word processing are more 'in sync' than thinking and writing. You think more quickly than you can write. You can learn (with practice) to word process much more quickly (70+ words per minute) than you can write (about 30 words per minute).

Real Life

Cari didn't like Math, and she hated her low marks, so she chose to drop Math in Grade 12. After a successful two years in community college, Cari decided to transfer to university and complete her B.A. in Psychology. To her horror, almost every university rejected her application because she did not have Grade 12 Math. Ultimately, she was forced to switch from psychology to sociology to get accepted. Once she got there, of course, she was shocked to find that she actually enjoyed Statistics!

Jennifer was focused on an Arts degree, and so decided against Physics in high school. Like many students, though, she changed direction part-way through and is now completing a Masters degree in Speech–Language Pathology (which is strongly oriented toward the sciences). Although she is doing well, a basic background and understanding in physics would have made a big difference and saved a lot of remedial effort.

David hated Math, and found endless ways to avoid programs where Math was an entry requirement. After three semesters at a community college, and two years in a distance learning degree program, he decided to transfer to his local university to major in History. Guess what he discovered? No Math, no acceptance into third-year History.

A

5. Volunteer. Investigate volunteer opportunities in your community and select one that offers you the chance to learn, grow and contribute. If you think you might want to work in Health Sciences, for example, explore the volunteer needs in your local hospital or rehabilitation centre. The idea is to experience different settings relevant to career options that interest you — this just might help you discern a great opportunity from your worst nightmare!

6. Research the world of work. There are lots of sources of information. As we've suggested, talk to everyone you can about the work they do. Most people appreciate being asked, and the insider tips you receive will be invaluable. When possible, visit people's workplaces to get an inside look. Read about careers that interest you — good material is usually available at university and college career centres, and at public libraries. Find out more about the work your parents do. Check out job-shadowing opportunities in your community: perhaps you can follow a journalist around for a few days, or a dentist, or a systems analyst.

 Nine Brilliant Things to do While You're in Grade Eleven

1. Continue to maintain good grades in your academic subjects (and if you have any doubt about taking academic subjects, see the real life stories above!). American colleges and universities will include your Grade 10 and 11 grades when assessing you for admission. Continue to keep your options open.

2. Keep up your volunteering and athletics. Be strategic — be sure these activities complement your academics and do not negatively affect your grades. Remember, you are unlikely to be selected to a university on the basis of your athletic achievements alone. At the same time, it is important to be a well-rounded student and to demonstrate a variety of skills.

Check to see if your community operates a Youth Volunteer Corps (YVC). They will help you find a placement at a not-for-profit organization doing volunteer work that will interest and challenge you. Otherwise, consider approaching churches, service clubs

(Rotary, Kinsmen), hospitals, nursing homes, seniors lodges, the Humane Society, environmental groups, theatre groups, food banks, the Crisis Line, and the local Immigrant Aid Society. Also, check your local newspaper and other community publications for volunteering opportunities.

You might create your own opportunities: shovelling snow for a senior neighbour; visiting a shut-in; befriending someone with special needs and participating with them in outings, swimming, games, or movies; working for a local politician; doing errands for someone in hospital. Whatever your choice, volunteering will boost your resume. It will show your work experience, highlight your skills, and showcase you as someone who contributes to your community. Not only that, you'll feel good!

3. Research colleges and universities. Use the Internet (relevant searches include http://www.yahoo.ca or http://www.baxter.net/educnet), check the academic calendars in your school's Guidance Office, or contact local colleges and universities. Write directly to select universities and colleges for their calendars and admission information.

4. Participate in more job-shadowing opportunities, and continue to talk with a variety of adults about their work. Ask questions like...
- How did you get into this field?
- What do you like/dislike about your work?
- What do you see yourself doing in ten years?
- Would you choose this field again?
- Do you have any advice for me?

5. Arrange to take the Scholastic Aptitude Test (SAT) this year (or early in Grade Twelve) if you want to consider studies in the United States. Ask your Guidance Department at school for application forms, or use the information in our "Extra Smarts" to contact the American College Board directly.

6. Use the summer to do upgrading or get tutoring if you are concerned about your grades. Check out the special summer programs for high school students that are offered by some universities.

7. If you are travelling, schedule some campus visits to get a feel for the university and its situation. Make it a habit to visit the local university wherever you go.

8. Research scholarships, your eligibility and how to apply. There are web sites available, or you can request booklets from any University Scholarship and Bursary Office. (Suggested web sites are listed in Extra Smarts.)

9. Consider a special summer program. There are a lot of great options if you have the time and resources. (Some of our favorites are listed in Extra Smarts at the back of this book.) Do your research — not all summer programs are created equal!

Lots of Brilliant Things to do While You're in Grade Twelve

You are now entering the "home stretch." This is a great — and potentially overwhelming — time. Stay calm, follow your schedule, and ask for help or support from your family, teachers and friends. You will survive! You will come out ahead!! You will probably even have fun!!!

1. Maintain your good grades, and sharpen those that may have slipped. Get some tutoring, if you need it, early in the school year. Use those good study skills (or if you didn't quite develop them yet, start now!).

2. Continue volunteering, if you can spare the time. When you experience a time squeeze, reduce your hours.

3. Talk to students who are already attending university or college. Ask about their experiences.

4. If you have not already done so, write away for University Calendars and Admission Packages from the schools that most interest you, or download information from the university's web site. Make copies of the application forms, so that you can do an application "rough draft." Note the deadlines for applications for each school. Collect all the documentation you will need to complete the applications, and keep it in a special file folder or a box. This will include your Birth Certificate, Social Insurance Number, and transcript application forms (for your final school grades).

5. Research the residences and their entry criteria. Complete the application forms. Pay attention to the deadlines!

6. Complete all the application forms and mail them in plenty of time to beat the deadlines (usually in January of the year you plan to attend). Include your interim grades, if required.

7. Apply for scholarships before the deadlines. Consider applying even if you do not fit all the criteria. Sometimes scholarships have few applicants.

8. If you are uncertain about a career direction, consider doing some career planning. Check out available career planning services at school, or at your local college. You may also want to find a psychologist specializing in Career Planning for Students. (Alternatively, write to us for information on our career planning workbook: *Career Smarts™: A Career Planning Workbook for Students*. Our contact information is at the back of this book.)

9. In April, be sure to obtain your Student Loan Application Forms from your local college or university. Read the section on student loans in this book.

10. By April, some schools will send you "conditional acceptance" letters. Don't despair if you haven't heard back from all schools. Some take longer. If your grades are questionable or borderline, you may be accepted later (in June or even July), depending on the availability of places in your program.

11. How to accept and reject. Rank your choices. If you get accepted by one of your lower choice schools, accept it and then reject it later, once you have heard from schools higher on your list. Be strategic!

12. Complete your final exams. If your final grades are an improvement on those you submitted with your application, you may improve your chances for late acceptance.

13. Enjoy your graduation celebrations and be proud of your success and accomplishment.

14. Find a summer job.

15. In the late summer, check out your campus of choice, and learn to find your way around the bookstore, the Students Union, eateries, the gym, and so on. Most universities have orientation programs for new students. Plan to attend. Get familiar with the place before the hordes descend! Choose a roommate and a place to stay. Register for your choice of first year classes and be sure to meet the deadlines (much more on this later in this volume).

16. If you are going to university or college and are staying at home, plan to review your status with your parents. Will you contribute toward room and board? Will you have the use of the car? What are your — and their — expectations?

17. Move in. You have arrived at Day One of your first year as a college or university student. Good Luck!

High School Planning Schedule
Countdown I
GRADE 10

☐ Choose academic courses. Keep options open.

☐ Volunteer.

☐ Research the world of work by talking to people.

☐ Develop good study skills and habits.

☐ Polish language and communication skills.

☐ Keep up word processing skills.

☐ Participate in athletics, debating, drama, art, music.

NOTES:

A

High School Planning Schedule
Countdown II
GRADE 11

September

☐ Continue to choose academic courses. Maintain your grades.

☐ Keep up volunteering and athletics.

October

☐ Research colleges and universities on the Internet.

☐ Look through university calendars in school Guidance Office.

November

☐ Write away to selected universities for calendars and admission packages.

☐ Participate in job shadowing opportunities.

January

☐ Study for SAT, if you plan to go to school in the United States (may postpone until later in year or early in Grade 12, if appropriate).

March

☐ First opportunity to write SAT.

☐ Research scholarships and write for information and application forms.

May

☐ Prepare for exams. Good luck!

July—August

☐ Upgrade courses, if necessary.

☐ Attend University Summer Program for High School Students (if appropriate).

☐ Get a summer job.

☐ Visit selected university campuses, if travelling.

High School Planning Schedule
Countdown III
GRADE 12

September

- ☐ Keep up good grades. Get tutoring help, if necessary. Use good study skills.

- ☐ Continue volunteering.

- ☐ Consider doing some career planning. Use *Career Smarts™*. Or, find a career planning service offered by a psychologist.

October

- ☐ Final college/university research on the Internet.

- ☐ Write for calendars, if you haven't already done so.

- ☐ Get residence application forms.

- ☐ Make copies of all application forms.

- ☐ Collect all relevant documents.

November—December

- ☐ Use section on Applying to University or College.

- ☐ Complete applications for admission and for residence.

- ☐ Prepare supporting documents.

- ☐ Include interim grades from Fall term.

- ☐ Apply for scholarships.

- ☐ Follow all instructions carefully.

January

- ☐ Mail all applications to meet deadlines.

April

☐ Apply for Student Loans, if you are eligible.

☐ Watch the mail box for conditional acceptance letters. Respond: accept or reject.

May—June

☐ Prepare for final exams.

☐ Write exams.

☐ Graduate and celebrate!

July—August

☐ Find a summer job.

☐ Expect late acceptance letters.

☐ Check out campus.

☐ Choose a roommate and place to stay.

☐ Register for first year courses.

September

☐ Start college or university. Good luck!

Keep this book close by for easy reference, as you navigate your way through college.

A Final Note — Taking a Year Off

Michelle wanted to travel in developing countries, and to help people in difficulty. After researching her alternatives, she connected with an organization that sponsored volunteers in small villages in Guatemala. She did her research carefully, and raised the money to pay her own way. The experience enriched her life, provided invaluable opportunities to discover her talents and skills, and strengthened her sense of self. It also helped her choose a career (directing field operations for non–profit organizations). She is now studying for a degree in administration, and continuing her Spanish language classes.

Many students tell us they feel "burnt out" after high school, and are not particularly motivated to start a college or university program. At this point, it is a good idea to step back and consider your options. You can probably expect your parents to be skeptical. They may fear that once you are out of the "learning loop" you will never return, and they know that will put you at a disadvantage.

Some of you may be concerned that your college or university will regard you as frivolous if you take time out, and may not accept you when you decide to apply. You, too, may have doubts about what will happen to your motivation for university, once you have had a taste of the working world. Of course, that is always a risk. Yet many students find that they are more than ready to start their studies after a year or two — particularly if that time is spent in a low paying, dead end job!

Many colleges and universities encourage you to take a year off between high school and university, particularly if you are unsure of your career goals. Educational institutions know that a motivated student will usually do well. Taking a year off has some real advantages. It allows you to clarify your career goals, to experience the work world, to earn some money, and to develop maturity and life skills.

Some of you may decide to travel — visit other countries, learn a new language, experience life from other perspectives, develop survival skills and meet a variety of different and interesting people. Sometimes, interesting situations present themselves as alternatives: working on a political campaign, spending time on a co-operative, participating in the Armed Forces Reserves. Opportunities to participate in student programs overseas may also appeal. We encourage you to explore these options (and again we include some of our favourites in Extra Smarts). A cautionary note: these programs are often expensive, although you may qualify for scholarships or other financial assistance.

You will undoubtedly find that a year off will mature you enormously. Professors report that their best and most motivated students are those who have taken time off to do some growing and get some life experience.

Perhaps time off is a good option for you, too.

College is not necessarily the next step after high school. Many students feel pressured, exhausted, bewildered, fearful of making poor choices, and unmotivated. None of these feelings is necessarily permanent. A year off is a healthy alternative. If your client is a reluctant student, she may well end up with mediocre grades, withdraw, and feel she has failed. On the other hand, when she is motivated, enthusiastic and engaged, she will be a good student.

You and your client can look at other options together:

- *Identify her skills and talents (using the checklists and your own observations);*
- *Look at the alternatives available that will be a good match;*
- *Encourage volunteering as an opportunity to contribute, learn, grow, network;*
- *Remember that your client's choice is not a permanent commitment. It may mean 'buying time' to make good future choices, as well as saving money for a while longer.*

Or try this approach: Ask your client to imagine that the financial 'tap' has been turned off. There is no money available for college. If he goes, he will have to finance himself. Any choice he makes will have your support. Now ask him to develop a plan for himself. He may include options like applying for loans and scholarships, taking time off to work, working and studying part-time. This exercise may help you gauge his current commitment to, and readiness for, university.

Another approach is to suggest that your client plan a perfect year for herself, with no financial or parental constraints — except that she may not attend college. Together, you can then look at the activities she comes up with, how important they are, and how they could be translated into real possibilities.

Hannah wasn't sure what she wanted to do with her future. She'd also had enough of school and wasn't ready for university. Instead, she found two part-time jobs, lived at home, saved her money and went travelling for part of her "year off." By the end of that year, she learned a bit about life — and had enough of low-paying jobs! She still wasn't completely decided on a career, so she enrolled in General Studies at university. She explored her interests further, and then choose a fruitful career direction.

part two:

Get Set: Choose Smart

A) KNOW YOUR INSTITUTIONAL OPTIONS

Our purpose now is to guide you through the process of deciding where you will go to school. We will start with the broad question — what type of educational institution is right for you? Then we will focus on the more specific questions — which institution will you choose, and how? First, then, what are your options?

Option 1: What is a University and Is It for You?

A university is a post-secondary institution that has the right, under provincial and federal law, to grant you a degree. A university's goals include: preparing students for various professions; providing a setting for academic study and learning; adding to the current body of knowledge through systematic research; setting and maintaining high standards in the learning process; and equipping students for life-long learning.

Which Students are Most Suited to University?

Because the university's goals are so diverse, it has the capacity to satisfy a broad range of personal goals as well. For example, at a university you may prepare for a highly specialized technical profession and at the same time study a variety of other topics and courses.

Students who succeed at university usually have a desire for, and a commitment to, academic learning. Successful university students enjoy (at least most of the time!) reading complex material; analyzing data critically; researching and writing reports and essays; studying independently; managing time well in response to a demanding work load; and building excellent oral and written communication skills. Most have a desire to develop and challenge themselves, to explore new ideas and attain new levels of excellence.

B

What are the University's Admission Requirements?

1. Subject Requirements

Many university programs require you to have completed specific high school subjects, and at a certain level (for example, English 30). Some may also require essays, portfolios, interviews and/or personal information sheets. Obviously, it is extremely important to check out these requirements, so that you can take the appropriate subjects during your high school years. Consult individual university calendars for the specific requirements of the programs you are targeting.

2. Mark Requirements

Each university or college calendar may specify a general minimum average for admission (for example 75%). In certain high-demand, limited-enrollment programs, the mark requirements for admission may be even higher. Mark requirements can also vary from year to year, depending to some extent on student demand for specific programs (sometimes programs in high demand will set higher minimum standards). Again, check the current, specific requirements for your program of choice.

3. Out-Of-Province Applicants

If you wish to apply to universities outside your home province, you should consult the calendars for admission requirements and procedures. Procedures and requirements often differ from province to province. At the risk of sounding like a broken record, don't get caught uninformed!

4. Mature Student Applicants

If you are a "mature student" and do not have the published admission requirements (for example, a high school diploma), you may still be considered for admission on an individual basis. The age for determining mature student status varies from age 21 to age 23 across Canada. Again, check the calendars of the universities you are considering. When universities evaluate mature student applicants, they are interested in your potential to handle the university program selected. As a result, you may be required to take some upgrading courses, particularly in English and Mathematics.

Please be cautious! We can discuss admission requirements in a general way, but specific requirements will always vary from province to province, from institution to institution, and from year to year. You will need to request information directly from those institutions of interest to you, at least 18 to 24 months before you plan to attend.

What are the University's Educational Opportunities?

1. Undergraduate Studies

Undergraduates (students in the process of earning their first degree) typically spend three to four years — and sometimes up to five years — earning a Bachelor of Arts (B.A.) or a Bachelor of Science (B.Sc.) degree. The B.A. or B.Sc. is a general academic degree (sometimes described as a "liberal arts" degree); it is not intended as preparation for a specific profession. You may require a B.A. or B.Sc. in order to pursue a professional degree, a graduate degree, or as a fundamental credential in many occupations and industries.

Other undergraduate offerings at the university include co-operative education programs, which mix salaried work terms along with academic terms and are generally spread over five years (see our section on co-op education for more details). Many universities also offer international exchange programs, in which students take a full or partial academic year at another university, often in Britain, Europe or the United States, and now also in Japan or China.

2. Professional Undergraduate Studies

The primary alternative to a B.A. or B.Sc. is a professional degree — that is, one which will prepare you to work in a specific profession. Programs leading to a professional undergraduate degree (such as engineering, nursing, physiotherapy, law, social work, or education) usually begin with a general educational background based on the liberal arts and/or sciences. Sometimes this means you need a B.A. or B.Sc. first, and sometimes not — that depends on the profession and the university. Then the professional degree adds specialized education and training.

You will be taught, and learn to apply, the skills and problem-solving strategies specific to your professional specialty. You will be exposed to the profession's standards of behaviour and code of ethics. You may also be required to complete a licensing exam and/or a period of internship before you are formally admitted to the profession. (Some of these procedures are governed by the profession's licensing organization, rather than the university.)

3. Some Traditional Professional Undergraduate Programs (all offerings highly dependent on the individual university!)

Admission available after required high school preparation:
Agriculture • Business • Commerce and Finance • Education • Engineering • Forestry • Journalism • Landscape Architecture • Nursing • Nutrition • Occupational Therapy • Pharmacy • Physical Therapy • Social Work • Survey Science • Translation and Interpretation • Urban Planning

Admission available after one to two years of university:
Business • Education • Occupational Therapy • Optometry • Physical Therapy

Admission requiring the completion of an undergraduate degree:
Architecture • Arts Administration • Business Administration • Dentistry • Education • Health Administration • Law • Library Science • Medicine • Museum Studies • Social Work • Psychology (Clinical, Counselling, Industrial, School) • Speech Language Pathology • Theology • Translation

4 . Graduate Studies

You can enroll in Graduate Studies only after you complete some or all of a first (undergraduate) degree. Examples of Graduate Degrees include: Master of Arts (M.A.), Master of Science (M.Sc.), and Doctor of Philosophy (Ph.D.). University teaching positions, as well as many research positions in universities, government, business, and industry often require a B.A. or B.Sc. (3 to 4 years), followed by an M.A. or M.Sc. (1 to 3 years with a thesis), followed by a Ph.D. (2 to 3 years with a research dissertation).

UNIVERSITIES

Advantages	Disadvantages
• Opportunities to gain a wide range of knowledge in a variety of subject areas.	• A minimum of 4 years of study.
	• A bewildering number of courses to choose from.
• Preparing for a professional career, requiring a Bachelor's degree, like Engineering, Teaching, Nursing, Physiotherapy and others.	• A very competitive environment. You need to maintain good grades to pass.
• Obtaining a Bachelor's degree to gain admission to Graduate Schools for Law, Medicine, Business, Architecture, Speech Language Pathology and others.	• Each course contains a lot of material to learn, perhaps more than you are prepared for.
	• Bachelors of Arts, Science and Social Science degrees do not lead directly to careers. They are educational, rather than career specific. You may need further training at a college or technical institute.
• Broaden your educational base by being exposed to new knowledge areas and leading edge research.	
• Professors very knowledgeable and well-educated.	• Most expensive educational option. Fees are higher than those at colleges, and you will spend 4 years, instead of 2.
• Some employers still see a university education as more credible than one from a college.	• Very big classes (often over 200) in the first two years.
• Some employers specify a university education, because they believe you will have learned how to think and problem-solve.	• Everything is BIG—more students, more buildings, more professors, more classes, more confusion, more distractions, more choices, more work.
	• Often, very impersonal. Need to look for sources of help and support.
	• Teaching may not be geared to under-graduate students' needs. Many professors are more research-focused than teaching-oriented.

B

onsultants

Following are some questions to ask yourself:
- *When you were 18, did you go to university or college?*
- *What were your goals?*
- *Did your parents encourage and support you?*
- *What were the outcomes for you?*
- *Why do you want your child to get a college or university education?*
- *How has your past experience (at university, or not) shaped your present attitudes?*
- *How will you feel if your child chooses not to go to university or college?*

Then there are some questions to talk over with your client:
- *What do you expect to gain from university?*
- *What do you hope to learn?*
- *Where do you see yourself seven years from now?*
- *Is your vision a good match with university life?*
- *Are your expectations likely to be met?*

Option 2: What is a Community College and Is It For You?

A community college is a post-secondary educational institution with one primary goal: to provide *job-related* programs of instruction that combine theoretical learning with practical experience. Community college programs sometimes include work experience opportunities or field placements. They may also include one or more salaried work terms, as part of a co-operative education program.

Some colleges offer classes in high school subjects, enabling students to pick up the courses they lack for admission to certain programs. Many colleges also offer the equivalent of first and second-year university courses. These may be accepted for credit at university. (Before enrolling in such courses, you should of course be sure that they will be accepted for credit by the university of your choice.)

Some colleges are also starting to offer three or four year degree programs in specific applied and professional fields. For the most part, these are degrees not available in nearby universities. They are also degrees that are closer to the college mandate of combining theoretical learning and practical experience. For instance, Mount Royal College in Calgary, Alberta offers degrees in Applied Small Business and Entrepreneurship, and in Applied Communications.

What Students are Most Suited to College Programs?

- Students who wish to acquire the specific knowledge and skills that employers are looking for, in the hope that this will lead to employment directly after graduation.
- Students who have investigated the available options and know what specific program they want to take, and why.
- Students who have the commitment and drive to acquire training and expertise in a specific job-related field.
- Students who may choose to continue their education at university after a more gradual introduction to the academic environment, and especially students who do better in smaller classes with more instructor attention (this can include mature students, young students, part-time students, and students from smaller communities).

What are the typical College Admission Requirements?

Normally, college applicants must have a high school diploma. Mature students without a high school diploma will usually be reviewed on an individual basis; some upgrading may be required before you can begin your selected program. Your marks will be relevant, but the requirements are generally not as stringent as at a university. Criteria other than marks are often considered during the admission process. For example, you may need to provide a portfolio of drawings for admission to an art-related program, or you may need to participate in interviews and show evidence of volunteer experience for admission to a social services program.

What are the Educational Options at Community Colleges?

At the completion of most college programs, you will have earned either a *diploma* or a *certificate.* Colleges will offer diplomas or certificates in many job-related fields, the names of which will vary from institution to institution. Typical fields of study include:

- Applied Arts
- Health and Community Services
- Creative and Communication Arts
- Science and Technology
- Business Studies

In each program, the required courses are designed to equip you with the *skills and knowledge necessary for job entry in your chosen field.* You may also have the option to choose from a variety of elective courses, either to create a specialty within your chosen field or to pursue topics of personal interest. In addition, some colleges offer general arts and science programs, which allow students to try out a variety of subjects and explore personal interests more closely before selecting a specific job-focused program.

Most full-time diploma programs are two to three years in length. Most full-time certificate programs can be completed in one year or less. Diploma and certificate programs may also be available on a part-time basis, through evening and weekend programs. Of course, a part-time program will take more years to complete. Typically, the college's general calendar will provide information on full-time day programs. Part-time and evening programs are usually described in the college's continuing education calendar.

In addition, most colleges offer non-credit, career-oriented courses and general interest courses, also usually in the evenings through the Department of Continuing Education. Finally, as we have mentioned above, most colleges have programs in fields such as the arts, sciences, business, communications, and the social sciences, which can be transferred to a senior university to complete a degree.

Hints

Pay attention to the differences between degree, diploma, and certificate. Know what you are working towards. A degree is typically awarded after the successful completion of three to four years of university. A diploma is usually awarded after two years or ten full courses at a community college or institute of science and technology. A Certificate is usually awarded by technical institutes, colleges and universities for successful completion of up to five full courses of study. It is often pursued as a first step toward specific qualifications, or as an additional learning experience after a degree. There are also many exceptions to these statements. Ask questions and be informed!

Kelly graduated from university with a B.A. degree and a major in English. Then the search for a career began — for a lively, energetic, outgoing person who enjoyed working with people. After some research, Kelly decided she wanted to work in Public Relations. She enrolled in an Applied Communications Diploma program at a community college. There she developed the practical skills which ultimately led her to a Public Relations and Marketing job with the local newspaper.

Early in Grade 12, Jodi was keen on going away to university. She was ready to "spread my wings and experience life," she told her parents. Jodi and her parents took a trip to the university she was considering. They toured the (rather large) campus; checked out classrooms, lecture halls and library; took note of eateries, residences, and recreation facilities; and asked dozens of questions. Probably most importantly, Jodi got a chance to experience the pulse and energy of the place — students hurrying, chatting, buried in books, lining up at cafeterias and copy machines, filling classrooms, working on computers. It felt like a bustling — and somewhat overwhelming — city. Would she be ready to leave home for this big, anonymous campus by next year?As a result of that experience, she checked out the local university and community college options. Ultimately, she decided to start at the community college in her city, and select courses that would transfer to a senior university. Once she had completed her first year, she would have more confidence in herself, and would feel more comfortable moving to a university away from home.

A Final Note: What is an Agricultural College?

Traditionally, agricultural colleges have trained people to enter the fields of farming and agribusiness. These colleges have a long and distinguished history in Canada. Over the years, as the field of agriculture has become more complex, agricultural colleges have risen to the challenge by offering a wider range of educational and training programs. This evolution is reflected in the mission statement of one such institution: "We are a responsive, innovative and client-centered educational organization dedicated to excellence in careers education, adult development, applied research and services, primarily in the areas of Agriculture, Horticulture, Land Management, Applied Business and Environment." (Olds College, Olds, Alberta). There are about twelve colleges in Canada offering a full or partial range of agricultural courses.

COLLEGES

Advantages	Disadvantages
• Shorter programs, usually 2 years.	• Not all courses are transferable to a senior university.
• Less expensive. Fees are generally lower than for university, and for a shorter time.	• Employment opportunities are often restricted to entry level, unless you continue to upgrade.
• Smaller classes and more individual attention.	• Salaries for graduates are, on average, lower than those for university grads, but higher than for high school grads.
• Instructors' main focus is on teaching.	• May require an extra year of study, if you transfer to university to complete a degree (i.e. 5 years, instead of 4).
• Programs are geared toward specific career and occupational skill development.	• Two-year diplomas in Arts and Science are not useful, on their own, for getting a job.
• High school upgrading courses often are available.	
• University courses (particularly first 2 years in Arts, Sciences, Business and Social Sciences) can be transferred to a senior university.	
• Some Applied Degrees are granted after 3 or 4 years of study, without transferring to a university.	
• Supportive to mature students.	
• More personal environment, smaller classes, more student resources.	
• Good first step towards university.	
• Larger number of graduates find career-related jobs.	
• Many part-time/evening programs for working students.	
• Co-op programs available.	

Option 3: What is an Institute of Science and Technology, and Is It For You?

Institutes of Science and Technology train students to be skilled technicians, technologists and tradespeople. These institutions are becoming the schools of choice for more and more students. They offer hands-on, relevant training that equips students to find work in our technically-advanced world — training that is often high tech and in high demand. In the words of one institution's mission statement: "We are committed to equipping people to compete successfully in the changing world of work by providing relevant, skill-oriented education. We achieve this by ensuring we meet the skill requirements of employers . . ." *(Southern Alberta Institute of Technology Calendar,1995).*

Institutes of Science and Technology tend to offer programs that are shorter than colleges or universities. Some programs can be completed in three to six months,while others take one to two years. Many students with university degrees also turn to "technical schools" to develop the technical competencies they need to become employable. In fact, more university graduates are currently enrolling in technical schools, than technical school graduates are enrolling in universities.

In addition, technical schools provide various trades with the academic components to their apprenticeship programs, and some offer upgrading courses in Math, Chemistry and Physics for those apprentices who need additional courses. Some apprenticeship students will then continue on to university to earn a degree. In other cases, the technical school may be able to grant a three or four year Applied Degree in certain programs, so that transferring to university is no longer an issue.

INSTITUTES OF SCIENCE AND TECHNOLOGY

Advantages

- Less expensive tuition fees.

- Shorter, usually 2 years, although some programs are 6-12 months.

- You gain specific hands-on, skill-oriented training—in demand by employers.

- Learn technical skills that are up-to-date.

- Add them to a degree to become marketable, by having practical skills.

- Learn the theoretical components to apprenticeship programs.

- Upgrade math and science skills.

- Some institutes now offer Applied Degrees, and reduce the need to transfer to university for a degree.

Disadvantages

- They offer few academic courses in Humanities, Arts, Languages.

- Not all programs are recognized by universities for transfer credits.

Many universities do not, as yet, accept technical school graduates on transfer by giving credit for their previous studies. This is slowly changing, as schools of all stripes are being forced to share shrinking financial resources co-operatively. Check the specific requirements of any program you are considering.

What Will My Teachers Be Like in Various Educational Settings?

At University: *You can expect to be taught by a professor — generally someone who has a Ph.D. and is academic and research-oriented. Some professors are highly committed to being good teachers, and some are much more committed to their own scholarship and research. Graduate students, who are pursuing Masters or Doctoral degrees, will often assist the professor by teaching labs and tutorials, and by marking exams and assignments.*

Colleges: *College instructors are usually more focused on teaching, and assisting students to learn, and less focused on their own scholarship and research. Instructors are often hands-on professionals, who bring their practical knowledge and work experience into the classroom.*

Technical Schools: *Institutes of Technology employ practical, experienced, highly-skilled technical and trades instructors, who teach you "what you need to know" from their own experience and knowledge. They are journeymen, or work in the field they teach.*

The New Integration:
How a "Hybrid" Might Work for You

Universities and colleges have had to do a great deal of
re-thinking about the programs they provide. Provincial
governments are reducing funding, demanding better
planning and expecting more creative utilization of
institutional resources. All of this has required that
educational institutions become more co-operative,
more open-minded, and less protective of their "turf."

As a result, educational institutions (especially colleges,
universities and technical institutes) are looking at new
ways to integrate programs, improve communication
with one another, and generally cooperate more
effectively. Sometimes this means a new structure for
working together — such as the Metro-Halifax
Universities Consortium in Nova Scotia, which facilitates
coordinated courses and shared resources among the
seven universities in the Halifax area. Other times this
means a brand new institution — such as Seneca in York,
Ontario, a hybrid which will offer studies in unique
disciplines like Applied Chemistry, Early Childhood
Education, and specific aspects of Communications.
Often the goal is to combine the analytical and the
technical aspects of knowledge in an improved offering
to students.

For several years, Alberta and British Columbia have
encouraged their universities to develop stronger
alliances with community colleges, enabling easy
transfer with credit from college to university. In some
program areas, students can earn a degree from the
University of Victoria or the University of British
Columbia without ever leaving their community college.
In another example, the Okanagan University College
has become an independent, comprehensive "university
college," offering a range of undergraduate degree,
diploma, vocational, developmental, career, health,
and technical programs at its campuses throughout
the British Columbia interior.

One of the latest of these innovative developments is the
Technical University of British Columbia in Surrey, B.C.
TechBC, as it is known, is expected to fill an important
niche as it offers students the opportunity to do applied
research in co-operation with business and industry.

Students can earn graduate and undergraduate degrees as well as diplomas and certificates in applied programs and professions. TechBC will partner with other educational institutions and offer classes via the Internet, as well as through multi-media, on-campus classes, and at regional learning centres.

In another example, the Southern Alberta Institute of Technology (SAIT) in Calgary is developing agreements with three universities in Alberta to take graduates from SAIT and allow them to complete degrees (usually two extra years) at a senior university. SAIT is also becoming involved with high schools, offering advanced technical courses to high school students and thereby "fast-tracking" them into technical careers.

This type of innovation is the current trend. Within a few years, we believe the majority of educational institutions will be sharing resources and offering creative "hybrid" programs. The potential certainly exists for meeting the needs of students, and the employment marketplace, more effectively.

This is also a time for caution and careful evaluation. Many of these new, innovative programs are still "ironing out the wrinkles." Carefully research the credentials which you can expect, and be cautious about anything requiring the use of new technology — there are always growing pains. Be sure you get the education or training that you signed up and are paying for! Our advice...

- Read the program literature carefully.
- Ask lots of questions about how courses are offered, taught, evaluated, and what will be expected of students.
- Talk to graduates who have completed the programs, if there are any, and ask for their opinions of the benefits and pitfalls.
- Make sure you have the required computer software and hardware, including a modem, so that you can access on-line classes, information, tutorials, and so on.
- Check with potential future employers — if you have done your career planning ahead — to gauge their impressions of the program you are considering.
- Evaluate and compare costs, time frames, and convenience, with those of traditional programs.

Alternative Training Options

Option 4: Co-op Education
Learning and Working
at the Same Time

Co-op education offers you an academic program
integrated with a period of time in the world of work.
Co-op degrees have been offered for a number of years.
Two of the pioneering universities in this field were
Simon Fraser University in Burnaby, B.C., and the
University of Waterloo in Ontario. The smart side
of co-op degrees is that they provide you with an
opportunity to build career-related work experience
while you learn. You add the benefits of a supervised
work component to your academic program.

Over forty universities and colleges provide co-operative
programs, allowing you to alternate academic and work
semesters. Naturally, these degree programs take longer
to complete, but there are enough advantages to make
them a worthwhile choice for many students.

CO-OP DEGREES	
Advantages	**Disadvantages**
• You get paid for work semesters, which can ease financial pressures. • You may learn new technical, financial, sales, marketing and research skills. • You have an opportunity to develop communication and interpersonal skills. • You will get practice in organizing, planning and problem-solving skills. • You have a chance to become a team player. • You develop a network of people who may help you in your future career. • You may get a foot in the door with an employer.	• Your degree will take longer to complete. • There is a great deal of competition for placements in co-op programs. • Many programs select only the top students. • You may be required to find your own work-term placement. • You may not always receive good on-the-job supervision or training.

Many universities tend to concentrate their co-op programs in the sciences (Physics, Geology, Biology, Math, Chemistry), as well as the applied sciences and technology (Engineering, Computer Science). Others focus more on Business and Management. Some universities have shown great creativity and diversity in their choices of co-op programs: Mount St. Vincent, the University of Toronto, the University of Calgary, and York University are good examples. They have developed co-ops in areas where it is not always easy to find course-related work experience. Look to these universities for co-op programs in such diverse fields as: Information Management, Tourism and Hotel Management, Social Work, Arts and Media Administration, Philosophy and Religious Studies.

An interesting variation on the traditional co-op program is the route taken by the University of Windsor. It has developed agreements with the University of Detroit Mercy and other universities in Michigan. Students in many departments have access to courses, research facilities and library resources at other institutions, as well as to field placements and internships. Law students attend classes in Windsor and at Detroit Mercy, and are able to sit for their Bar exams in all states. This joint Law program has created the first Commercial Trade-Dispute Center dealing with the North American market. Similar arrangements are continually being forged by schools interested in cooperating with each other.

Academic education and work experience are also integrated in internship programs. The difference is often one of timing. Co-op work terms are usually interspersed with academic terms. Internships, on the other hand, usually happen at the end of one's academic program. Internships may last from six months to a year, and are often the final requirement for graduation. Some enterprising universities have created internship programs for their graduating students in career areas ranging from Computer Science, Journalism, Drama and Political Science, to Music Therapy, Communications, Engineering and Psychology.

Co-op and internship programs continue to grow, as both students and employers recognize their value. Check university calendars and web sites for current information.

Option 5: What is Apprenticeship, and Is It for You?

Are you interested in learning a trade? If so, the path of an apprentice may be perfect for you. Students who choose this option seek out and work with a qualified employer — one who is willing to provide the on-the-job experience and guidance necessary for you to be certified in a trade. Most apprenticeship programs are in the construction and industrial fields, but there are other options. You might become a hair stylist or a cook this way. For most programs, you must be at least 16 years old and have completed grade 10. Many employers will also expect a high school diploma. Solid language and math skills are important.

Some students choose to cross-train, learning more than one trade by the apprenticeship route. This increases your flexibility and value to an employer.

Generally, an apprentice signs a two- to four-year work contract and must register with the provincial Apprenticeship and Trade Certification branch. Provinces are continually revamping apprenticeship programs, so we encourage you to check with your local Apprenticeship Board for up-to-date information. This is also an area of innovation. In Alberta, for example, it is now possible to start your apprenticeship before you finish high school — and complete both at the same time. The province is offering a Registered Apprenticeship Program (RAP) that enables young people to earn apprenticeship and high school credits at the same time. Students study full-time while working toward trade certification; one hour of study counts as both an hour of apprenticeship and an hour toward a diploma.

Not for Males Only...

Young women are more inclined to consider apprenticeship than ever before. Women in the trades report better pay and higher job satisfaction than those in many traditional "women's jobs." Working in the trades has built confidence, financial independence, and personal well-being. For many women, this is a terrific route to owning and operating a successful business.

Trade Satisfaction...

According to a 1996 survey published by the Alberta provincial government, nine out of ten apprentices and journeymen are happy they chose a career in the trades. Surveyors reported that:

- people who complete apprenticeships are twice as likely to be self-employed as other members of the workforce;
- over 70 per cent of those surveyed were still working in the trade they apprenticed in, and 48 per cent were either supervisors or managers;
- over 70 per cent of respondents would recommend their trade to friends or family.

APPRENTICESHIP TRAINING

Advantages	Disadvantages
• It's the recognized way to learn a trade and earn your journeyman's papers.	• Often, you will need to find an employer who is a qualified journeyman, before you can enter the program of your choice.
• It is a practical, hands-on training program: learn as you work/work as you learn.	• You may have to wait to get into a specific course, if the program is popular, or over-booked. (Hint: get onto the wait-list and be flexible about start dates.)
• You earn a wage while you work, and your wages increase each year, as you pass your exams and move to the next level.	• You need to buy your own tools, protective clothing, and books.
• Many programs are supported, to an extent, by government funding.	
• Some programs help to match you with suitable employers.	
• Courses are usually scheduled throughout the year.	

B

**Private Vocational
and Technical Schools
(Where Students Pay to Be
Trained for Paying Jobs)**

If you are the sort of person who likes to get straight to
the point, you may be a good candidate for a private
vocational/technical education (usually called a vo-tech).
These privately-owned schools offer pure, lean training
programs that can usually get you into a paying job
within a year, sometimes two. Private vo-tech
institutions tend to skip over academic subjects unless
they are directly necessary to the work you are seeking.
These schools emphasize instead the solving of everyday
work problems, and the development of specific skills
needed on the job.

Most private vo-tech institutions aren't cheap. Costs run
from about $800 for a nine-week program such as
manicuring, to more than $6000 a year for longer
programs such as computer science. In some provinces
(Alberta, for example), student loans are available to
those attending recognized private vo-tech colleges.

Why would you spend the money for a private school
when you can learn the same job skills in a less
expensive public vocational-technical school, or in a
community college? Good question. Here are some of
the pluses of private vo-tech training.

Advantages of Private Vo-Tech Schools:
- Some students choose the private route for one basic
  reason: they need specific job skills, and a job,
  quickly. These students want job training, not
  academic enlightenment.

- Vo-tech schools offer enrollment throughout the
  year; you need not wait until the semester break or
  until September. Because these schools offer short-
  course units, with almost instant feedback on
  achievement, students who didn't do well in high
  school may find their first experience of
  accomplishment in a vo-tech classroom. This feeling
  of success may be as important as the content of the
  course in preparing to work at skilled jobs.

- At some vo-tech schools, a performance evaluation policy permits you to leave when you know the material. Under this "open exit" philosophy, if you can pass the test — for instance, tune an engine — you can leave immediately as a graduate rather than wait out the full term. (Check with the schools you apply to.)

- Vo-tech classes are usually small and instructors may give extra attention to individual students. The institution does not like to see students drop out, sometimes because a drop-out is a lost sale.

- Private vo-tech schools are usually quite concerned about their placement records and business reputations. They must satisfy their customers, and their provincial governments, or eventually they will go out of business. Staff generally work hard to place graduates, and to cultivate the esteem of local employers. Many vo-techs claim high graduate placement rates (over 85% of graduated students).

Disadvantages of Private Vo-Tech Schools:
- One drawback to private vo-tech study is that the school may not have the extensive classroom, laboratory and recreational facilities that a government-supported college does. If you are considering a private vo-tech course requiring hands-on experience with various tools (for example auto mechanics or dental assisting), be sure to check whether you will be learning on up-to-date equipment. Of course, you should also check with potential employers as to whether they recognize the course you are considering.

- Beware of "dream schools," institutions that feed on individuals chasing unlikely dreams in glamour careers. The never-ending stream of would-be stars has spawned an industry of dream merchants who operate schools for actors, artists, authors, baseball and basketball players, comedians, disc jockeys, models, musicians, race car drivers and songwriters. They will take your money, but they rarely deliver on overly-hyped promises.

- Very, very few courses at a private vo-tech school will transfer for academic college credits. You may eventually want a university degree. This will leave you having to start again at the beginning.

- The best private vo-tech schools can provide the skills you need to get good jobs and to advance more quickly. In other cases, unscrupulous operators promise high-paying jobs and rosy futures that they cannot deliver. If you don't want to be fleeced, do your homework checking out the school. Start by asking if the school is accredited by the Provincial Department of Advanced Education.

Choosing A Private Vo-Tech School:
- Check the advertising. A school's advertising should communicate that students are being sought, not employees. Ads recruiting "trainees for immediate openings" are ambiguous and misleading.

- Watch out for guarantees. Avoid schools that guarantee you a job, insist that there's "a place for you in _____ field," or suggest you'll be anything other than a trainee after graduation.

- Beware of hype. Resist pressure to sign an enrollment agreement quickly in return for reduced fees. You're looking for quality training, not just a bargain. Often, the so-called discount is a myth.

- Read the fine print in the enrollment agreement regarding payments and tuition refunds if you drop out. For instance, if the agreement says you'll get a refund if you withdraw because of an emergency, check out what "emergency" means. Will you get a refund if a parent becomes ill and you must quit to work full-time, or is an emergency refund given only if you become ill? Ignore verbal assurances from a school's representative. Get clarifications or modifications to the agreement in writing.

- Request graduate placement figures. What percentage of graduates find jobs related to their studies? Remember, though, you have no accurate way to verify a school's publicized placement rate.

This is why it is important to contact recent graduates. Ask for a dozen names and try to get in touch with four or five. If at all possible, interview former students face-to-face.

- Ask employers for their opinions. Use questions such as: Would you hire graduates from this school? Have you hired any during the past few years? Were they hired because of the training they received at this school? Did the training make any difference in their starting salary?

- Talk to current students, privately if possible. Ask if you can visit the school and speak to students on a random basis. See how people evaluate the training they're receiving.

- Clarify graduation credentials. Because vo-tech schools specialize in specific job fields, they do not give academic degrees. When you complete your program, the school will give you a certificate or diploma confirming your newly-learned skills. Find out if completion of the program qualifies you for independent certification if that is relevant to your field (as it often is in cosmetology, real estate, veterinarian assistance, or telecommunications electronics, for example).

One More Possibility? Distance Learning

Since the mid-1970s, there has been significant growth in what is called "alternative" or "non-traditional" or "external" or "off-campus" education. All these are ways and means of obtaining an education without sitting in classrooms day after day, year after year. This method of earning a university degree (especially the bachelor's degree) typically requires you to cover the same material that is covered in the classroom — including writing term papers and passing mid-term and final examinations. Students usually work from a course study guide, as well as from textbooks and in some cases audio tapes, video tapes, CD ROMs, educational TV programs, and the Internet.

Distance learning is particularly useful for those students who are unable to quit their jobs and travel to a distant city to engage in a four-year undergraduate university program. By enrolling in a distance learning program, such students are able to work on a degree at their own speed, while continuing to work at a full-time or part-time job.

Although at least seven Canadian universities offer correspondence courses to students, two institutions, Athabasca University and British Columbia Open Learning Agency (Open University), were established specifically to provide students from across Canada with an opportunity to obtain university degrees via distance learning. At any one time, there are approximately 15,000 students enrolled in courses at Athabasca University. For more information, or an academic calendar, you may write or e-mail either institution. For the relevant addresses, as well as other universities offering distance learning options, consult our Extra Smarts.

Distance learning in the United States is very well established. For more detailed information, we suggest you purchase a copy of Bear's Guide To Earning College Degrees Non-Traditionally, by John and Mariah Bear. Dr. Bear has spent many years researching and publishing this guide; the comments on each specific university are well worth considering. The Bears are strong advocates of non-traditional modes of study.

R eal Life

Les had one accounting course left before he could graduate as an engineer. Because he had plans to work overseas, he enrolled at Athabasca University and his accounting course went with him. As he completed assignments, he faxed them back to his instructor. He also used fax and e-mail for instructor consultations. He was able to write his final exam by special arrangement, through the local university in the city where he was working.

R eal Life

Cody is pursuing a creative writing degree through Carleton University, while he teaches English as a Second Language in Korea. He relies on e-mail to correspond with his instructors and to complete his assignments. In this way, he has been able to work, travel and continue his education.

We will now shift our focus to talk about what goes on inside a university, college, or other post-secondary institution. The first thing you encounter when you start to look inside is an entirely new vocabulary. The first thing we will do, therefore, is talk about some terms. These may seem confusing, or the distinctions may appear mundane at this stage. Don't worry. Treat this as a ready reference section — take a look through it now and then digest the pieces as you need them later. Believe it or not, these words will become as familiar as eat, drink, sleep and learn as you progress through the next few years...

**The Calendar
(not the January through December kind) —**
If you are considering a Canadian university education, you have about seventy institutions to choose from. Each of these institutions has a calendar. (Community colleges and institutes of science and technology also have calendars.)

The calendar is where you find everything you ever wanted to know — and an incredible amount of detail that you won't believe you need. The calendar will tell you what disciplines and professional programs the university offers. It will provide information about the town or city where the university is situated. You will learn how large the faculty (teaching staff) is, and whether the course selection offered has enough variety for you. Use the calendar to check admission requirements (courses, marks, and so on), as well as the closing dates for applications. (That bit is important. Universities and colleges rarely, if ever, accept late applications.) Graduate students are frequently required to take additional entrance exams. This information is also available in the university calendar.

**General Bachelor of Arts (B.A.) or
Bachelor of Science (B.Sc.) —**
These are the basic undergraduate degree programs, usually requiring 3 years of full-time study during which you will take the equivalent of 15 full-year courses (or 30

half-year courses). At many universities, these degrees will require 4 years of study and 20 full-year courses. In a four-year program, the first year is usually an opportunity to explore a wide selection of courses, without the need to choose a major field of study. This first year is often called a "General Studies" year.

Undergraduate student — This is what you are called when you are working towards your first degree.

Graduate student — This is what you are called when you are working towards a graduate degree. To get to this stage, you must have earned a bachelor's degree and then decided to continue your education.

Term or Semester or Quarter — This is a segment of the academic year. The regular school year is made up of two terms — Fall (September to December), and Winter (January to April). Some universities have a Spring term (May and June), and a Summer term (July and August) during which a limited number of full-time courses are available.

Course — This is a unit of academic study that is either one term in length (half course) or two terms in length (full course). Courses are given names, numbers and credit value, depending on the particular university's system, e.g. BIO 210 (3). Directions for interpreting the course name and numbering system will be provided in the university's calendar.

Credits — You need a certain minimum number of credits to graduate, depending on your program of study and your institution. You earn credits by completing courses. Most half courses (one term) are worth 3 credits; full courses are worth 6 credits. Courses with a lab component are often worth 4 or more credits. (The credit values may not be the same at all universities.)

Program — This is the selection of courses leading towards a degree. You must fulfill all the requirements of your program before you can earn your degree. Some courses will be compulsory in a particular program of study, while others may be optional or elective. Programs will often specify different types of courses you must choose from, such as the requirement to take a certain number of humanities courses, or science courses, or senior level courses.

Compulsory/ Elective — A compulsory course is one you must complete in order to fulfill your program. An elective course is one you choose to take, for general interest and/or for its relevance to your studies. Your program will likely require that you choose a certain number of electives, in addition to the compulsory courses. Both compulsory and elective courses "count" towards the requirements for your degree.

Major — A major is the academic subject area you choose to study most intensely in a your degree program. This choice is called "declaring" a major. Examples of majors include psychology, sociology, physics, chemistry, English, criminology, and so on. You will take more courses in your major discipline than in any other subject area. Some universities expect five to six full courses to complete a major. Students may also select a double major, for example sociology and psychology, or chemistry and physics.

Minor — This is a subject area selected as a secondary discipline of interest by students in an honours program or other four-year program. A minor is usually four full courses. It is not necessary to declare a minor.

Honours B.A./B.Sc. — This is an undergraduate degree that usually requires an extra year of study beyond the normal three- or four-year degree program. Honours students take 9 or 10 full-year courses in a particular subject area or discipline. More often than not, there is a high minimum marks average you must achieve in order to be accepted and maintain your place in an honours degree program. You may also be required to complete a special research and writing project called an honours thesis.

Discipline — This term is used to describe a specific subject area, for example English, political science, philosophy.

Faculty — This is a division within the university that includes many departments specializing in various related disciplines. For example, the Faculty of Arts contains the departments of English, philosophy, classics, and so on, while the Faculty of Science will include the departments of chemistry, physics, biology, zoology, and others. The Dean is the person who is in charge of a Faculty. Under the Dean are several Chairmen in charge of each of the departments.

Lectures, Tutorials, Science and Language Labs, Seminars — Unlike high school, instruction at the university or college level is not an 8:00 a.m. to 3:00 p.m. matter. Depending upon your program and status (full-time or part-time), you may attend as many as twenty hours of class time a week, or as few as ten hours. That certainly won't be all the time you'll need. Although "out-of-class" time requirements vary greatly, a good rule of thumb is to expect three hours of homework or preparation time for every hour you spend in class.

Lectures — The lecture is the basic unit of instruction at a college or university. Usually taught by professors, lectures are given two or three times a week and often last for either 50 or 75 minutes. Expect lectures to be very impersonal. In the arts and sciences, for example, you will probably be in a class of somewhere between 60 and 300 students. In some first-year or second-year classes, you may find yourself sitting in a lecture hall and watching your professor on a television screen, while he or she lectures to a full lecture room next door or down the hall.

Tutorials — The tutorial is a complement to the lecture, and is usually taught by a Teaching Assistant (TA). Tutorials are designed to supplement the professor's work, offer you individual attention, and allow you to ask questions and discuss reading assignments. Your lecture class will be broken up into several tutorial sections, each of which will be much smaller than the full lecture class. This is a great chance to interpret your learning and test your own views. The TA may ask you to complete weekly assignments based on the lectures. Often, a percentage of your final grade will be based on tutorial performance, so it is wise to treat the tutorial seriously.

Language and Science Labs — Language labs are designed to help you with your accent, pronunciation, expression and utilization of language. Science labs allow time for vital hands-on experience, such as experiments and dissections. Labs are an important practical component in classes such as biology, statistics, or physics.

Seminars — Seminars are usually given only in the third and fourth years, as well as in graduate courses. They are designed to give upper-level students the opportunity to give detailed presentations of material they are researching. Class members comment, discuss and make suggestions, based on their own research and reading.

Grade Point Average (GPA) — This is the system for calculating your average grade that is used by most (although not all) universities. Your GPA is a grade score calculated out of a total of 4. The GPA system converts letter (not percentage) grades. You will receive a letter grade for each course. The GPA allows the letter grade to be converted to a numerical value. The average of those values can then be calculated, for a semester, a year, or your entire degree. GPA values will vary; a typical distribution would look like this:

$$
\begin{array}{rcl}
A & = & 4.0 \\
A\text{-} & = & 3.7 \\
B\text{+} & = & 3.3 \\
B & = & 3.0 \\
B\text{-} & = & 2.7 \\
C\text{+} & = & 2.3 \\
C & = & 2.0 \\
C\text{-} & = & 1.7 \\
D\text{+} & = & 1.3 \\
D & = & 1.0 \\
F & = & 0
\end{array}
$$

Academic advisors — These are university staff that assist you in deciding program majors and course selections. They will help you ensure that you meet all the requirements of your program. Sometimes advisors are available to talk to students prior to their admission to the university. Know your program requirements — you can certainly make better decisions that way!

B

C) KNOW HOW TO MAKE A GOOD CHOICE (AND MAKE ONE)

Part 1: Do the Footwork

Your education is one of the most significant investments you will make — an investment of time, energy, passion, brainpower, and of course money. At the other end of this investment are the rewards you are seeking — a new set of skills and abilities; an understanding of how to think and process and learn; lasting and important relationships; a highly increased capacity to earn and contribute in the world. Along the way is a powerful stretching and growing experience.

In other words, the stakes are high. You want to make a good choice. You need to find the educational opportunity that offers the best fit for you, given where you are now and where you want to go. Our goal is to support you in the process of making that choice. And we believe the best choices are *informed decisions*.

So we will give you lots of homework! There is research to be done, information to be collected, important questions to be asked. We will provide the framework. You will need to put it into practice. These are the first steps into a great adventure.

The good news is you have already made a great start. Remember "Know Yourself' and "Know Your Career Options" from Part I of this book? Education planning, as we have said, begins with career planning. Career planning is the organized, systematic process of:

- *exploring* your personal abilities, skills, interests, values, work-style, and personality;
- finding potential "good fits" by *researching* the world of work, its demands, requirements and rewards; and then
- *choosing* the appropriate education and/or training to take you where you want to go.

Hints

"If you don't know where you are going, you'll probably end up somewhere else."
– David Campbell

The "GET READY" section of this book has helped you make good progress with steps one and two of this list. In the "GET SET" section, we are working through step three. So far we have considered several institutional options for pursuing your education, and have introduced you to some new terms. Now we will coach you to get the specific, detailed information you need to make your informed decision.

 Informed Decision Step One: Read Plenty

All academic institutions publish several sources of information, ranging from the general introductory to the highly detailed and specific. Here is some of what you should look for:

You may need to spend some more time with the material in Part I of this book. Or you may be looking for a more detailed examination of the career planning process. If the latter is true, we invite you to work through our companion book, Career Smarts™: A Career Planning Workbook for Students. Further information is available at the back of this book.

- *Admission guides for first-year students* — usually take the form of pamphlets that outline degree programs, admission requirements, typical first-year programs, residence and housing information, extra-curricular activities, campus visits, and who to contact for further information.

- *Pictorial brochures* — will provide photographs, campus maps, and people on campus to contact.

- *Program-specific brochures* — will vary with each institution. For example, a university may publish brochures on each of its faculties, brochures on each of its colleges and/or residences, brochures on unique programs, brochures about scholarship and awards information.

- *Student handbook* — will be published by the students' council to provide everyday, useful information. Where are the cafeterias and off-campus eating spots? What social activities are available? When do public buses run?

- *Web site on the Internet* — will offer a wide range of data and trivia. You can usually find all sorts of program-specific details, and also get information on clubs, facilities, recreation and contacts. (More on this below.)

- *Calendars* — are the ultimate source of information, including detailed admission requirements, programs, degree requirements, course descriptions, university regulations, marking systems, appeal procedures, and so on. It is critical to be able to find your way comfortably around a university calendar, *before* you fill out an application. (More on this below, too.) Some calendars are "on-line," others are only in paper. (American universities often call this source a "catalog.")

Research on the Net

Use the World Wide Web (Yahoo Canada, for example) to investigate schools which might interest you. Once you have narrowed down the field, you can always write for more detailed information and application forms.

- Look carefully at the school's offerings and requirements.

- Check to see if your programs of interest have prerequisites, and whether you can complete them as part of your program (e.g. some community colleges offer high school upgrades in Math, English and Sciences).

- Check the school's social activities and events, and the clubs you might join.

- Read (if they are available) some of the student newspapers, which are usually published weekly and will offer you some insight into the culture of this institution.

Get the Calendar and Use It Well!

Any educational institution will send you its calendar for a small fee, usually around $5.00. If you are in high school or community college, it is likely that your guidance counsellor or school library has a collection of these calendars (at least for the universities and colleges in your province). If you are applying from overseas, consult the nearest Canadian Consulate or Embassy, or write directly to the institutions that interest you. Most libraries across Canada, including university libraries, stock calendars from the major or best-known universities in Canada.

When you first start consulting calendars they may seem very confusing, no matter how well they are designed. You will need determination and the courage to ask questions when you don't understand something. The payoff will be access to a wealth of useful information. How to proceed:

- Keep the terms and definitions section in this book handy.

- Work from general information to more specific information. Read to get a sense of the institution before you start trying to understand the rules for declaring double majors. Use the *Calendar Information Sheet* we provide below. Complete one sheet for each institution you would like to research.

- Sometimes calendars are not well designed. Make careful use of the Table of Contents and the Index. Look for the headings listed on our Calendar Information Sheet. You may want to consult a course advisor and/or team up with a friend.

The table on the following pages will be a great help in pulling the information you need out of the calendar. Do this for each of the institutions that really appeal to you; the process will help you decide where to apply.

CALENDAR INFORMATION SHEET FOR COMPARING PROGRAMS
(Make a copy for each university you are comparing)

Where

Name of university or college _____

Program title _____

Program length _____

Admission Requirements

Subjects required for admission _____

_____

_____

Subjects included in average for admission _____

_____

_____

Program

Purpose of the program _____

_____

Courses required per year _____

_____

_____

Number of hours of classes and labs per week _____

_____

P. 1

	Year 1	Year 2	Year 3	Year 4
Compulsory Courses				
Elective courses within the department				
Courses I like from other departments and faculties				
Course selections preferred				

P. 2

Scholarships/ bursaries	I will investigate the following:	When and how to apply
Residence	Names of residences:	When and how to apply
Other necessary information	I would like to know:	Who and where to contact

Follow-up

1. I will visit these campuses: a) _____

                                      b) _____

                                      c) _____

                                                   by _____

2. I will contact _____ at _____

                         _____ at _____

                         _____ at _____

P. 4

Informed Decision Step Two: Visit Personally

Reading is the right first step. However, no amount of reading will replace the sense of a place you get from actually being there. Of course, geography may make a personal visit to all your institutions of interest difficult. But there are probably some options within visiting range. Know that you are welcome, and that visiting and asking lots of questions is the right thing to do. Again, here are some of the possibilities:

School Fairs: When the University comes to you...

Sometimes high schools invite representatives from universities and colleges in the area to visit, giving students an opportunity to ask for information first-hand. You are smart to take advantage of such opportunities. Go and ask lots of questions. Collect brochures and written materials. If you haven't heard of such an event at your school, approach your guidance counsellor or student council representative and suggest your school give this a try.

Sometimes universities send ambassadors across the country to recruit potential students. These representatives usually host an open house at a downtown hotel and advertise the event in the local newspapers. Once again, if the opportunity presents itself, go. Your guidance counsellor might receive advance notice of these recruitment tours — ask him or her to keep you informed.

A new concept — the first-ever Mega-University Fair — was recently staged by nineteen of Ontario's universities at the Metro Toronto Convention Centre. Taking their lead from the American style one stop marketing approach, the universities set up a giant information fair, which was attended by an estimated 40,000 prospective students and their parents. Its success may stimulate other provinces and regions to do the same.

Campus Visits: When you go the University...

Most universities offer "campus visit days," including tours given by senior students who are happy to answer your questions. Often, you can sit in on classes and talk to other students. Call student affairs to ask when such tours are scheduled. If the timing does not work for you, ask what other arrangements can be made. When you are travelling, make it a habit to drop in at the local university and at least get a feel for the place.

Campus visits can answer, or begin to answer, lots of important questions:

- What do I want from university in general and this one in particular?
- How will the program(s) I might apply for here help me achieve my goals?
- What does the university expect of me? Can I meet these standards?
- What facilities (residence, student centre, library) will help me if I come here?
- Does this university offer the specific programs I am interested in?
- Is this university well equipped? Well designed? Well maintained?
- Do I feel comfortable here? Can I imagine becoming a part of this place?

Most universities have offices that can provide:

- a campus tour,
- an interview with a program advisor,
- a visit to a class or lab, and
- contact with students enrolled in programs of interest to you.

When You Go, Use a Checklist!!

Following is an extensive checklist for collecting information about the institutions that interest you. There are questions for you to ask and observations for you to record. The checklist will focus your campus visit time, helping you get what you need to make your informed decision. Make a copy for each institution you are seriously considering. Take it with you when you visit, ask the questions you need answered, and record what you learn.

If a personal visit is not possible (maybe the institution in question is on the other side of the country), would a telephone interview with an advisor or senior student be an option? Perhaps there is someone you could arrange to chat with over the Internet. (In fact, the internet might act as a "virtual tour" of the institution.) Don't be afraid to ask the student advisory office for someone to talk with. Anyone involved – staff or students – knows the importance and complexity of this decision, and should understand your desire for information.

As with all such tools in this book, make this checklist your own! Use words, colours, symbols – whatever works to record your impressions and help focus your decision.

Consultants

Offer to visit the colleges that are of most interest to your client. Plan together what you will check out when you are there. Visit college fairs together, and interview college representatives (remember to let your student ask the questions). Collect the schools' brochures and calendars. Have a series of discussions or meetings to share your impressions and ideas. Use the checklists provided in this book, and fill in the lists separately for later comparison. As you work through this process, ask yourself about your own preferences. What motivates your preferences — is it prestige, cost, family tradition, your own interests? What are your expectations of a college education? How will you react if your client chooses a different college from the one you prefer?

DOES THIS PLACE APPEAL TO ME?
CAMPUS RESEARCH CHECKLIST

Here are some questions to ask and observations to make. Make copies of the next 3 pages to use when you visit each campus. You will get more from your visit, if you have read brochures and the calendar and can add the following information:

A. GENERAL IMPRESSIONS	NOTES
Size and ease in finding your way around.	
Location — is it part of the community, or set apart? Is this important to you?	

B. UNIVERSITY PROGRAM	NOTES
What areas of study are particularly strong at this university?	
Athletic programs available?	
Are computers (e.g. NoteBooks) required/encouraged as a learning tool?	
What areas of study are unique to this university?	
What work/study or co-op education programs are there?	
Are international exchange programs available?	
Class size – 1st year?	
Class size – upper years?	
What High School subjects are most important for success in program(s) you are interested in?	
Marks or GPA needed to enter, pass and/or continue in your program?	
Availability of academic advisors?	

B

How do they help?	
Library hours? Accessibility of information?	
Is e-mail utilized/provided on campus?	
Other	
C. HOUSING	**NOTES**
Availability of residence for 1st year students?	
Criteria for admission?	
How are room-mates selected?	
Cost? Are various types of meal plans available?	
Co-ed floors available?	
Single rooms available?	
Off-campus housing available? Cost? How close to university?	
Residence rules and supervision?	
D. TRANSPORTATION	**NOTES**
Public transportation? Costs?	
Cost and availability of parking (if required)	
Other	
E. STUDENT ACTIVITIES	**NOTES**
Range available— clubs, student government, political, athletic, special interest groups, etc.	
Are activities that are important to you available?	
What is the centre for student activity? How is it used?	

What orientation is there for 1st year students?	
F. STUDENT SERVICES	**NOTES**
What kind of health services are available on campus?	
Career and placement counselling centre—programs and services offered? How does it help grads obtain employment?	
Where can students go for help with personal concerns or crises? How available is it?	
What programs are there to assist students in the transition to university?	
G. QUESTIONS TO ASK OTHER STUDENTS	**NOTES**
Class size — personal experience and impressions.	
Availability of faculty for help — personal experience and impressions.	
Transition to university—personal experience—what helped?	
Social atmosphere—ease in 'fitting in.'	
What is most important in determining success at university?	
Is it better to live on or off campus?	
Are student orientation activities offered?	
Other	

B

Informed Decision Step Three: Know Your Criteria

Where do you want to live? What kind of school do you want to attend? What services and options do you want available to you? What is important to you in selecting a post-secondary institution? What will make you happy? This step creates a filter for screening your options. The choice of educational institution is an intensely personal decision. We can't tell you what is important to you. We can help you decide what's important to you, by having you think about the following questions...

WHAT DO I WANT MOST?

Place a check mark (✔) next to those factors which are important to you.

FACTORS	HOW AND/OR WHY IS THIS IMPORTANT TO ME?
1. LOCATION OF UNIVERSITY a) Capital city b) Large city c) Small city or town d) Staying in my own town/city	
2. NATURE OF UNIVERSITY a) Small (under 5,000 students) b) Medium (5-10,000 students) c) Large (over 10,000 students) d) Campus appearance & 'atmosphere' e) Other _____	
3. DIVISION OF ACADEMIC YEAR a) Semester system (2 terms for full-time study: Sep - Dec, Jan - April) b) Trimester system (3 terms available for full-time study)	
4. PROGRAMS/ADMISSION REQUIREMENTS a) Bilingual program/ courses available b) Co-operative education and/or other work/study programs available c) Admission requirements suit my interest and ability d) Admission average for program I want e) Range and flexibility in course selection within the program of choice	

B

WHAT DO I WANT MOST?

Place a check mark (✔) next to those factors which are important to you.

FACTORS	HOW AND/OR WHY IS THIS IMPORTANT TO ME?
f) Flexibility in changing programs after 1st year g) Other _____	
5. RESIDENCE/HOUSING a) On-campus housing availability for first-year students b) Availability and cost of off-campus housing c) Living at home	
6. SCHOLARSHIPS a) Availability of 1st year scholarships b) Will I qualify? c) Availability of scholarships beyond 1st year	
7. STUDENT SERVICES a) Special services for learning or physically disabled students b) Athletic facilities and programs c) Extra-curricular activities in _____ d) Assistance for students, especially in first year, in study skills, essay writing etc. e) Mature students services f) Other _____	
8. SOCIAL AND PERSONAL a) Parents' preference of university b) Friends' preference of university c) Near relatives d) Other _____	

WHAT DO I WANT MOST?

LIST THE MAIN FACTORS THAT ARE MOST IMPORTANT TO YOU

1.	
2.	
3.	
4.	
5.	
6.	
7.	
8.	

Informed Decision Step Four: Complete Your Own Process

You should be almost ready to complete some application forms. Check out your progress, and your process, by checking (✔) the following:

❐ Have you checked to see which universities offer the program(s) you want and what the admission requirements are? Are there any special requirements, such as interviews or portfolios, that you need to prepare?

❐ Have you checked the calendars of at least 3 universities of your choice and compared the programs? What courses are compulsory and optional in your program?

❒ Have you talked with a university representative, or better still, visited the campuses of 3 universities you plan to apply to — either in person or on the Internet?

❒ Have you attended any special events such as open houses, or attended a class?

❒ Have you talked with your school counsellor to see if your grades and achievements to date indicate that your decision is realistic at this time? If you are a mature student, you can talk to a student counsellor at the college or university you plan to attend.

❒ Do you know why you have chosen the program(s) you are selecting?
  ❒ What does it mean to you?
  ❒ Your family?
  ❒ Your friends?
  ❒ How is your choice related to your career goals?
  ❒ If your career goals are unclear at this point, will your choice provide the flexibility you may need?

❒ Do you know why you wish to go to university?
  ❒ How does it meet your expectations for yourself more than other possible options such as community college or on-the-job training?

❒ If you have selected a very competitive or limited enrollment program, do you have a back-up or alternative plan? (Essential for good mental health!)

❒ Have you investigated housing availability on or off-campus, and
  ❒ How and when you should seek accommodation?

❒ Have you done some financial planning and decided how you will finance your education?
  ❒ Do you qualify for scholarships, bursaries or government student loans?

MY DECISION MAKING PROCESS

A. The information I know, or have confirmed...

1. _____
   _____
   _____
   _____

2. _____
   _____
   _____
   _____

3. _____
   _____
   _____
   _____

4. _____
   _____
   _____
   _____

5. _____
   _____
   _____
   _____

B

B. Information I need or things I need to do.	How?	By When?	Done ✔
e.g. get calendars	*E-mail universities. Phone those without e-mail.*	*Nov. 15*	✔
1.			
2.			
3.			
4.			
5.			

C. Concerns and/or possible obstacles that might affect success at university

1. _____

2. _____

3. _____

4.

D. To deal with these, I will investigate...

1. _____

2. _____

3. _____

4. _____

I will talk to...

1. _____

2. _____

3. _____

4. _____

B

```
Possible solutions...

_____

_____


_____


_____


_____


_____
```

Part 2: Prepare Your Applications

Start this piece of the journey by knowing that the application process is a big job! You are not the only one who will be going slightly crazy with forms, photocopying, paperwork of all kinds, deadlines, rules, regulations, and the post office. This is the beginning of your "form completion" life! But the rewards are out there. You definitely cannot be accepted to the educational opportunity of your dreams if you don't apply.

Our job at this point is to offer every single tip we know to make this process easier. Here are some strategies to save you time and maximize your chances for acceptance.

1. Make a copy or two of each page of each form you need to complete. If you are uncertain, do a mock-up first and keep the original for your final version.

2. Have all your information handy: student ID number, birth certificate, citizenship identification (if necessary), financial information, transcripts of marks, Social Insurance Number, and so on.

As your student begins the application process, encourage her to track deadlines for applying to colleges, scholarships, and residence. Decide (with her) what she would like from you: A reminder? Help filling out forms? A system for staying organized? Chocolate chip cookies? Nothing? You both need to remember this is her responsibility. You are simply her consultant. She can decide what she needs from you. She also needs to deal with the consequences, whatever those may be.

3. Most people no longer have typewriters handy (remember them?). If you are one of those people, then print your forms neatly, clearly, legibly, and in ink. Use blue or black ink only. Avoid using "white-out" correction fluid, or crossing out mistakes.

4. Answer all the questions to the best of your ability. Try not to leave blank spaces. If a question does not apply to you, write N/A (Not Available or Not Applicable) in the space. This indicates you have read the question rather than skipped it.

5. If you need more space than the usual two or three lines to list previous programs, write "see attached sheet" and attach an extra page with the relevant information.

6. List any honours and awards, if asked.

7. Consider your non-academic activities and volunteer experience. Be selective in your list. If your leisure activities centre around "hanging out with friends," you will make a less favourable impression than if you participate in sports, drama, music, debate, or community volunteer programs.

8. Keep a copy of everything you send. Consider sending your applications by "double-registered" mail or by courier rather than the normal mail service — it is faster and more reliable. Although it is also more expensive, the initial up-front cost may save you money and aggravation (and perhaps a forfeited place) in the long run.

9. Faxes? E-mail? Use these if the university offers them as an alternative to the mail-in system. Although not all admissions offices are set up to handle applications electronically, most universities do now have online application and registration facilities.

Advice from the Admissions Office

- Academic results are the single most important criterion. School grades count.

- Not all school grades are considered equally. English, Languages, Math, and Sciences will often carry more weight than Physical Education, Drama, and Music — unless you are applying to major in those fields.

- Volunteer experience is becoming a criterion for selection to some programs (e.g. Social Work) at some universities. Activities that contribute to the quality of the community are important, as opposed to something like "collecting golf balls in the rough."

- Develop a "Plan B" in case your top choices don't work out. You may need to select an alternative program or a different university. Consider a two-year college program that will allow you to transfer to university to complete your degree.

- Prepare carefully for admission interviews, if your university program requires them. Practice with a friend. Greet the interviewer directly and shake hands firmly. Say less rather than more. Speak clearly, maintain eye contact, and fidget as little as possible. Be gracious and thank your interviewer when the interview is complete.

- Write your admissions essay with thought, care and originality. Not all schools require one. If it is optional, then write it. It may give you an edge.

- Apply to a number of schools in case you are not accepted at your first choice destination. Four to six universities should probably be enough — unless your grades are questionable in which case you may need more options.

- Arrange for appropriate references. Most undergraduate programs in Canada do not require them, but some do. Ask instructors/teachers who know your abilities, have seen your progress, and are willing to write a good reference. Give them the information they need to complete a good reference easily: a summary of your grades, test scores, achievements, and awards, stamped pre-addressed envelopes, and the required recommendation forms.

The last word on applications:
check every document for spelling errors or missing information; submit documents that are clean and without visible correction marks; make an excellent first impression.

Keep track of your application process using the Application Schedule Organizer that follows. Applying to university or college has many stages, each with different due dates. The Schedule Organizer will be invaluable in ensuring that you don't forget to do something important. Note the relevant due dates you are facing. Make it your policy to be ready ten days before each due date to allow time for mailing. Transfer each of these deadlines into your day-timer or calendar if you use one.

APPLICATION SCHEDULE ORGANIZER

(Use a separate Organizer for each school you are applying to)

Name of University _____

Address _____

Phone # ( ) _____ Fax # ( ) _____

✔ INFORMATION	DUE DATE	DATE SENT
❏ Complete Admission Application Form		
❏ Complete Transcript Requests		
❏ Payment for Transcript Processing		
❏ Payment for Application		
❏ Standardized Test Scores		
❏ Applications for Residence		
❏ Applications for Scholarships		
❏ Applications for Loans		
❏ Admissions Essay (if required)		
❏ Letters of Reference (if required)		

Writing Your Admissions Essay

This may or may not be a step that applies to you. Not all Canadian colleges and universities require essays for undergraduate admission, although they do for Graduate School. If you are applying to school in the United States, most colleges will expect essays for both undergraduate and graduate acceptance. If you need to write an admissions essay, following are the relevant helpful hints.

Some universities define explicitly what they require in an essay: topic, exact length, format, and so on. Others leave everything open. It is important that you follow the directions carefully. It is not unheard of for an essay to be discarded because it was a few lines longer than the requirement, or formatted incorrectly. Seven hundred and fifty words means exactly that, no more and only a few less. Double spacing means exactly that too — no fudging. Unless otherwise specified, use a twelve-point font size. Any variation from the rules is easily spotted (whether you think so or not!) and not acceptable.

Generally, the essay is an opportunity to bring your application to life, to transform it from "just data" to a word-picture of you. The essay calls for a personal focus on your ideas, your life and your feelings. It is not a formal research-style document. Nevertheless, it is still important to follow classic essay writing style. Use a strong first paragraph to get the reader's attention, and an effective closing paragraph to bring your ideas together.

Suggestions For Writing Your Essay:

- *Give yourself plenty of time:* start early, collect your ideas, read some examples (several useful books are available, particularly at university bookstores).

- *Write a rough draft:* then wait a day or two before reviewing and correcting it.

- *Ask for feedback from others on the content and style.*

- *Proofread your final draft:* do so several times, checking for spelling and grammatical errors. Ask someone else to proofread it as well, to catch any errors you may have missed.

- *Use a creative writing style:* a strong, opening sentence that grabs attention, humour, anecdotes, interesting observations, and an engaging, positive manner.

- *Be concise:* many schools will indicate the length they want. If not, be brief anyway. A good essay is often not a long one.

- *Be informal* rather than stodgy; be personal without being too chatty.

- *Be positive:* use an upbeat, optimistic tone, emphasizing positive rather than negative decisions, choices, feelings, experiences. Yet, be realistic at the same time. Keep a balance.

- *Mention your strengths* and one or two weaknesses. Indicate how you have turned your weaknesses into positives.

- *Be accurate:* check your essay carefully for any spelling or grammatical errors. Remember that Spell Check is not reliable; it does not catch words that are wrong as long as they are spelled correctly ("their" for "there" is a good example).

- *Write the essay yourself.* There are agencies, and individuals on the Internet, that will write an essay for you. However, most admissions officers can spot these "professional essays" immediately and will automatically reject your application.

Part 3: Response Time

Rank your choice of universities from first to last. Accept the first offer of a place, while you wait to receive the others. If the second offer is higher on your priority list, then accept it, and reject the first offer (politely and in writing). Should your top choice come up, then take that and reject the others. Some schools require a non-refundable deposit to hold your spot. You may need to forfeit those, in order to get the university you want.

What do you do if you are not accepted by your colleges of choice?

- Some institutions may put you on a waiting list. If a place opens up, they will call you. This may happen close to the beginning of the school year, so keep your options flexible (switch from full-time to part-time work).

- Check calendars to see if you are still eligible to apply at other universities as a late applicant. Perhaps you can get accepted at a community college and complete one or two years of a transfer program, before re-applying to university.

- Look at the feasibility of taking part-time courses at university and re-applying as a full-time student the following year.

- If your grades need improvement, consider upgrading at an adult learning centre or community college.

- Apply at a distance learning program (Athabasca University, University of Waterloo, University of Victoria, are examples). You can then transfer your credits to an on-campus university after a year or two, or continue to complete your degree, through distance learning.

- Consider the wisdom of taking a year off, and working or travelling, while you reassess your options.

B

- If you want to know why you have been rejected, contact the Registrar's Office and ask for feedback on your application and what they might suggest to improve your chances next year.

- Common reasons for rejection include: lowered grades; increased competition for limited spots; some selection criteria unfulfilled (volunteer work, poor interview); late applications.

Don't reject the first offer you receive. It may be the only one.

Cheryl was too late to apply as a full-time student, but was offered a chance to take two courses as a part-time student. Not wanting to forfeit a year, she obtained permission from the university to supplement her courses with one from the local community college and one from Athabasca University. At the end of her first semester, she had completed 4 half courses, and, as the university offered a second admission in January, she was able to continue her program there. If she had not been admitted in January, her Plan B was to take more courses, as before, and complete one year as a "Multi-institutional Student."

GO!!
Student
Smarts

3

A) MONEY SMARTS:
INVESTING IN YOUR EDUCATION

As you undoubtedly already know, post-secondary education is expensive! There are several options to consider as you make your financial plans — and the earlier you make those plans, the better. Once again, our aim is to help you make informed decisions. First, we will talk about the expenses you are likely to face. Next, we will consider some funding sources. Finally, we will look at the issues involved in working while you go to school, which is a financial necessity (and a tough time pressure) for many, if not most, students today.

1: The Costs Ahead: Know Your Expenses

Total costs for an eight to nine month academic year at a post-secondary institution start from about $4,500 for a community college student living at home. At the other end of the spectrum, a university student living away from home can expect to spend from $12,000 to $16,000 or more per academic year. (Take a deep breath and keep reading!)

Your basic academic costs will include tuition fees, books, and supplies. These will, of course, vary greatly from institution to institution and from program to program. From the college or university's perspective, tuition fees pay a portion of the cost of your education; government grants pay for most of the rest. Tuition costs vary, therefore, depending on the relevant provincial government's fiscal health and policy choices at any given time. Currently, tuition is most expensive in the Atlantic Provinces, Ontario, and Alberta, while Quebec boasts the lowest tuition fees. In most provinces, fees are rising fast — sometimes by over ten percent per year.

Books and supply costs are highly dependent on your program. For example, students in fine arts-related programs can expect high supplies costs — often $1000 or more per academic year. (Most campuses have Book Buyback Programs that reduce costs slightly, both by providing you the option to purchase books secondhand, and by providing a place to resell your books once you are finished with them.)

For those not living at home, on-campus residence and food costs for an eight-month academic year will be approximately $4,500 to $5,500. The cost may be lower for students living off-campus in rental accommodation, but this will depend on the availability of rental suites, rental rates in the community, and whether accommodation is shared or single. Personal expenses will also vary greatly, depending on the standard of living you are accustomed to and what you can afford.

Item	University Living away from home	Community College Living at home
Tuition and activity fees	$2,500 - $5,000 per year	$2,000 - $3,000
Books and supplies (can vary—higher for art-related programs)	$850 - $1,200	$850 - $1,200
Rent (shared, off-campus)	$2,800 ($350 per month for 8 months)	Living at home
Food	$2,000 ($250 per month for 8 months)	
Personal expenses (entertainment, clothes, gifts, hobbies—can vary)	$1,500 - $2,000	$1,500 - $2,000
Transportation - Local Visits home	$400 $1,500 - $2,000 (depending on distance, mode of transportation and frequency)	$400
Medical/dental expenses	$300 - $400	$300 - $400
Total	**$11,850 - $15,800**	**$5,050 - $7,000**

C

2: Financing Your Education: What are the Options?

The occasional student will have all the money he or she needs, in the bank, ready to pay the educational bills. (This is the very occasional student. Actually, we've never yet met one; the concept remains entirely theoretical.) For most Canadian students embarking on a post-secondary educational program, some or all of the following options will be important.

1) Government Loans: The Canadian Federal Government provides a majority of its funding support to students through the Canada Student Loans Program. As an undergraduate student, you are assessed on the basis of your financial need, and are eligible for loans covering up to 60 per cent of your assessed need, to a maximum of about $5,600 per academic year. (This amount can change each year.) Graduate students are often eligible for more money.

In your assessment, you will fall into one of four categories: dependent, independent, married, or single parent. A dependent, according to the student loan program, is someone who: has been out of high school for less than four years, working for no more than two years, and whose parents are assessed as able to provide at least partial financial support. If you fit the first two criteria, your parents will be expected to provide information on their income and the size of your family. These factors will partially determine whether you need help or not, in the eyes of the Student Loan program.

In order to be assessed as an independent, you will have been out of high school for at least four years, or working for two years, or have no parent or guardian to sponsor you. Single parents and married students will also be assessed according to specific criteria before they are approved for a student loan. The criteria include money from other sources (working partner, full-time job, employment insurance, social assistance) and child care needs.

Hints

If you don't have a job, or if you lose your job, it's very important to contact the Student Finance Board. They will assist you in postponing your student loan payments until such time as you have an income.

Carolyn worked part-time in a florist shop while she was at university. Because she lived at home and her parents' income was considered too high, she was not eligible for government loans. She approached her parents to help and together they drew up a contract; they would pay for her tuition and books while she was at university. After graduation, she would repay this loan at $100 per month as soon as she had a job. Carolyn's parents chose not to charge her interest on the loan. Rather, they wanted her to benefit from the experience of borrowing and making regular repayments.

Provinces have the option to "top up" federal government student loans with their own tax dollars if they choose. Some provinces do and some do not, and this changes over time. Provinces have their own criteria for top-up funding, including disability, and level of parental income. Maintenance grants may also be available to students who, because of special circumstances, are not considered to have "normal prospects" for completing their education without additional assistance. This could include students with disabilities, and single parents. These grants top out at about $6,000 per year, in addition to the regular student loan program.

You can apply for a student loan through the Student Finance Board of the province in which you live. Most high school, college and university Financial Aid Offices will have application forms available, as well as staff who can answer your questions. You need to apply by mid-May to be approved and receive funds for the following September. Most loans apply to full-time students (those taking at least three courses per semester), however some restricted loans are available to those studying part-time.

The most important thing to remember is that this is not free money! You will definitely have to pay it back once you graduate (or once you leave the institution, if you do not stay to complete your program). Interest on your loans will begin to accrue immediately after graduation, but you may not be expected to actually begin repayment until up to 30 months after graduation. (Please note that the repayment schedule can be changed at the government's discretion — don't take our word for it!)

2) Private Bank Loans: Over the past few years, several banks have made it easier for students to borrow money for school, particularly if the student has been unable to qualify for a government loan. Each plan is slightly different, but generally speaking a student can borrow up to $6,000 per academic year. Usually, the bank will require a co-signer (someone with a good credit rating who will commit to paying the loan back if you don't), although it is not necessary for you to have a credit rating or a job. Without a co-signer, you can expect the interest rate to be at least 2% higher than if you had a parent or guardian to guarantee your loan — if you are able to qualify.

Some banks will offer you a line of credit rather than a loan, which enables you to access funds at intervals throughout the year using a special credit card. The maximum you can draw is typically about $5,000 per academic year. The interest rate on a line of credit "floats;" that is, the rate moves up or down as bank loan rates fluctuate over time. The costs are therefore less predictable.

With private bank loans, it is important to consider that you will be paying back interest on the loan from the time you receive the money (e.g. on a loan of $5,000 at 9.5%, you would have to make monthly payments of $40 starting immediately). You do not receive the same grace period as you do with government loans. If you qualify for government funding, then use that; the government pays the interest until you have completed your studies.

3) Loans from Family: You may have grandparents or other relatives who have extra cash stashed away in investments, and they may be willing to invest in you. We suggest that you approach this in the same way as you would any other loan. Write up a contract, agree to the terms, and check with a lawyer to make sure you are all protected. Then, have both parties sign.

Treating a family loan this responsibly reduces the risk of different (and often diametrically opposed) expectations. You now have a negotiated business deal, with specific accountability that needs to be taken seriously. The contract also represents your commitment to repay the loan, rather than to "assume" that the money might somehow become a gift!

4) Scholarships: Scholarships are usually awarded based on the academic merit of the applicants. Sometimes, they are also awarded on the basis of financial need, minority status, or other criteria of importance to the scholarship sponsor — for instance strong community service, leadership ability, athletic prowess, or the pursuit of a particular area of study.

Scholarships vary in amount from a few hundred dollars to several thousands of dollars. They are often awarded for a student's full period of study. Of course, if the recipient fails to maintain the necessary grades, or violates some other scholarship criteria, the award will be withdrawn.

Finding the right scholarship for you will require some research. An excellent source of information on student scholarships is a series of books by Michael Howell, called *Winning Scholarships.* University awards officers also provide specific lists of scholarships that pertain to their schools. The Internet is now becoming a valuable resource for researching scholarships, and the information you find there is usually current. (Unfortunately, many print publications are not as reliable and are often out of date.) *Maclean's Guide to Canadian Universities '98* provides a detailed scholarship directory. This is a useful, current resource.

The How-to of
Effective Scholarship Application...

- Contrary to common mythology, you do not have to be utterly brilliant to qualify!

- You do, however, need to have reasonably good marks.

- Get involved in community and extracurricular activities. Volunteer from Grade 9 onwards if you have your eye on scholarship funding.

- Keep a record of your successes, awards, prizes and citations — for school, extramural, and volunteer activities.

- Check out clubs, churches, your parents' employers, and service organizations (e.g. Rotary) for sources of scholarship funding.

- Write a stunning essay, with an original slant.

- Start your applications early. You may need time to collect letters of reference from your teachers, and to write a good essay.

- As with any important paperwork, follow the instructions exactly. Draft your applications early and ask someone to proofread them. Be sure they are clean, error-free and completely professional.

- Keep trying! Scholarships are available throughout university, not just in your first year.

3: Putting it all together:
Getting Specific about What You Need

You may be at the cost comparison stage, or you may have decided on a program and be in the cost planning stage. You may have several living options to evaluate: residence versus home, residence versus off-campus rental, one city versus another. The following questionnaire will help you assess the full financial picture: what you need, where the money will come from, what questions are as yet unanswered.

Some of the information you need to complete this questionnaire will come from admissions brochures, university calendars, or your local Student Finance Board advisor. Other information might come from talking with students who have been where you're headed. The cost of living varies across Canada. Be as accurate as possible about the living expenses wherever you are headed. Use the questionnaire to guide your research – on tuition fees, residence costs, required supplies, living expenses, and so on.

HOW WILL I FINANCE MY EDUCATION?		
Resources	$	Comments
Loans	_____	_____
Summer earnings, after expenses (estimate)	_____	_____
Savings from previous jobs, gifts, etc.	_____	_____
Parents' assistance	_____	_____
Other - possible scholarships or bursaries	_____	_____
Total	_____	_____

WHAT WILL MY EDUCATION COST?

Before completing the chart below, check admissions brochures, calendars or talk with a counsellor at your local Students Finance Board office. After completing your research and obtaining information on tuition fees, residence fees, supplies for the universities and/or colleges you are interested in, fill in the chart below so that you can compare the costs of attending the various institutions. This should help you to compare the cost of residence versus living at home, residence versus renting off-campus, university costs versus community college, etc. Cost of living varies across Canada.

Item	Name of Institution	Name of Institution	Name of Institution
	_____	_____	_____
	Program	Program	Program
	_____	_____	_____
Tuition and compulsory fees	$_____	$_____	$_____
Books and other supplies	$_____	$_____	$_____
Housing: off-campus			
Rent	$_____	$_____	$_____
Telephone	$_____	$_____	$_____
Utilities	$_____	$_____	$_____
Food	$_____	$_____	$_____
Housing: residence			
Room and meal plan	$_____	$_____	$_____
Other food costs, (if food plan excludes some meals on weekends)	$_____	$_____	$_____

Transportation			
Local	$_____	$_____	$_____
Visits home	$_____	$_____	$_____

Personal expenses*			
Entertainment	$_____	$_____	$_____
Hobbies	$_____	$_____	$_____
Clothing	$_____	$_____	$_____
Gifts	$_____	$_____	$_____
Misc. - stamps, newspapers etc.	$_____	$_____	$_____

Medical/dental costs	$_____	$_____	$_____
Total	$_____	$_____	$_____

*Does this estimate reflect your current spending habits? Can this be reduced, if necessary, in order to help finance your education?

C

EXPENSES VERSUS RESOURCES

Where do I stand?

Total costs   _____

Total resources   _____

Shortfall?   _____

Can I reduce any expenditures? How? (for example, live at home?)

_____

Improve resources? How? _____

Will I apply for a government student loan and/or grant?

_____

Will I need to work part-time during the school year? If so, how much? Will it interfere with my academic commitments? _____

_____

WHAT NEXT?

Any new information needed?

❑ Scholarships?

❑ Bursaries?

❑ Government student grants and loans?

❑ Summer job search?

❑ Other?

Where will I go for assistance?

List	Phone numbers
_____	_____
_____	_____
_____	_____
_____	_____
_____	_____
_____	_____
_____	_____
_____	_____
_____	_____

C

4: The Working Student: Will that be You?

At this point, the squeeze between available funds and necessary (or desirable) expenses becomes clear. Student loans, scholarships, and parents notwithstanding, few students are able to complete a degree without earning at least some money to support themselves. Most of you will probably work, at least part-time. The next step, then, is to consider the alternatives and make an informed decision...

1. Work full-time, study part-time. If you are currently well-paid, part-time studies may be a good option, particularly if you are not in a great hurry to complete your program. (If you take a minimum of 3 courses a year, it could take you up to 13 years to earn a bachelor's degree.) If, however, you are currently not well-paid, and holding a degree would improve your earning potential considerably, you may want to establish that higher earning potential as soon as possible. In that case, you may consider...

2. Work part-time, study full-time. In this case you will be poor for a shorter period of time (say five years), and then enjoy greater earning potential. You can expect to meet your occupational and financial goals sooner. However, you might also have student loans to repay, so build loan payments into your calculations.

3. Full-time job, full-time study is a challenging option that some students work hard to manage. You need to be a well-organized, careful planner to make this happen. Excellent time-management skills and efficient study strategies will be essential. For most, social and personal commitments will have to be minimized. Careful course selection, to accommodate both work and study schedules, is also essential. Be aware that tight scheduling will likely reduce your course options.

4. Working in the summer is, of course, the popular student option. You have the time available to earn a full-time salary for four months of the year. The key here is to budget your earnings wisely, investing in the coming year of education rather than a summer spending spree. You may still work part-time during the school year, or you may not need to if your summer earnings are strong and your spending is smart.

5. Take a year away from studies and work to save enough money to support yourself when you go back to school. You might do this before you start your program of study, or halfway through if need be.

Wherever and whenever you are working, it's useful (although not always easy or even possible) to take a job that has some relevance to your studies. Think of it as creating your own co-op program, where learning at work complements learning at school. (This can be a benefit to your employer as well as to you.) For example, maybe you can work in the accounting department of a company while you are studying Business Administration or Finance. Or perhaps as a nursing student you can find a part-time job in a nursing home.

If you do actually register in a co-op program, you may find that you can earn enough money during your work terms to ease the financial load. Co-op work terms are usually paid at the going rate for entry-level positions in the field. This may allow you to "just study" during your academic terms.

"What about my marks, if I work part-time?"
Research on working students indicates that those students with part-time jobs (less than 15 hours per week) do no worse than students who do not work. In fact, working may actually enhance some of your study strategies: you learn to manage your time, organize yourself, plan ahead. However, it is also true that students working more than 15 hours a week are at risk of earning grades lower than what they are capable of.

5: Once you have the money, Be Smart About It!

The last point we want to make about your money is that whatever the source of your cash flow, you will need it to cover some very specific (and considerable) expenses throughout the academic year. No doubt we are not the first people to suggest that you build a budget! But the truth is that $4,000 at the beginning of the year seems like a lot. By January, when you are facing your second round of expensive book-and-supply buying, it can seem like a lot less. Where does it all go?

Use the budget worksheet that follows to plan your income and expenses for the academic year. Now is a great time to do this. You've just completed your research, you're thinking about money, and you have what you need to finish the planning job!

MY BUDGET WORK SHEET

INCOME	SEP	OCT	NOV	DEC	JAN	FEB	MAR	APR
Family Support								
Summer job								
Part-time job								
Student loans								
Scholarships								
Other								
TOTAL INCOME								

EXPENSES	SEP	OCT	NOV	DEC	JAN	FEB	MAR	APR
Tuition								
Students union and other fees								
Text books and supplies								
Rent/residence costs								
Utilities								
Telephone								
Cable TV								
Sub-total								

C

	SEP	OCT	NOV	DEC	JAN	FEB	MAR	APR
Groceries or residence meal plan								
Entertainment								
Clothing								
Toiletries								
Transportation/ gas								
Parking								
Weekend and holiday travel								
Loan interest payments								
Personal computer								
Furniture, bedding, dishes, etc.								
Personal property insurance								
Moving expenses								
Other								
Sub-total This page								
Sub-total Last page								
TOTAL EXPENSES								

The next big decision you face is to choose what, specifically, you will study. Which courses are of greatest interest? Which are most important? What topics are you going to embrace, several days a week, for several months at a time? The menu is long and sometimes confusing. In this section, we aim to give you the criteria to make good choices. Then we'll talk about some of the other activities which you may want, or need, to make time for...

Step 1: How Many Courses?

Your first question might be: "Do I want to be a full-time or a part-time student?" Full-time students usually take a minimum of 3 courses and a maximum of 5 courses per semester (although many universities and colleges define 5 courses per semester as a full course load and anything less as part-time). If you follow the 5 course per semester route, you could finish your degree in 4 years of fall and winter semesters — or your diploma in 2 years.

The reality for many students is that a 5-course semester is a lot of work, particularly if your study skills are under-developed or if you have other commitments, like a job. Part-time students usually take 1 or 2 courses each semester. This may be the best way to transition from the workforce to college or university. Part-time students may also choose to work during the day and attend classes at night.

To make a good choice for yourself, it is important to look realistically at your schedule, your learning style, and your other commitments (work, family, training, athletics and other individual life situations).

Here's an example that might give you some clues to your own decision-making... Jenny is a good all-round student, who has to work smart and consistently to maintain good grades. She has a part-time job that pays for tuition and books and provides hands-on experience for her future career. She plans to apply to Graduate School to become a Speech Language Pathologist. In order to be accepted into Graduate School, she needs to maintain a strong GPA (Grade Point Average) of over 3.5.

She also needs to maintain her job to finance her studies. Given her circumstances, she chose to take 4 courses per semester, fall and winter, for 5 years — and to take on an additional 4-month full-time job in the summers. This allowed her enough time to keep up her grades, earn some money, and balance her life. She had to weigh the advantages of a lighter course load, excellent grades and a good part-time job with the disadvantages of an extra year at university.

First-year students sometimes take on more than they can handle. The temptation is to try doing it all and still doing it well. Our suggestion is that you take 4 courses in your first semester and monitor your progress. If you find you can handle an increased workload, then step up to 5 courses the following semester. You might also remember that you can make up courses during the spring and summer, if you need to, by combining your summer job with evening classes. (Note that summer courses are condensed into six weeks. You have to be prepared for classes twice a week for three hours each.) Some workplaces may also allow you flex-time, to accommodate your class schedule.

The options for part-time student life are actually becoming quite creative. Commuters on British Columbia's mainland, travelling each morning from Mission to Vancouver, can take a class from Capilano College on the train! Instead of reading the newspaper, they assemble in the last car and participate with their instructor in a college course on Current Events. This experimental class-on-rails will be expanded, if there is a demand for it.

The University of Calgary now offers a new way to study part-time. Weekend University was launched in 1996 to provide opportunities for working students to earn an interdisciplinary Bachelor of Arts or Science degree on Saturdays. Memorial University, in conjunction with the Newfoundland and Labrador Provincial College, now offers a joint business course on the World Wide Web. And nearly 20,000 students sign on to the World Wide Web to access courses through British Columbia's Open Learning Agency, which coordinates courses from post-secondary schools across British Columbia.

Hints

Some scholarships require that you complete a full course load (5 courses) in the previous year in order to qualify. Consider the requirements for any scholarship you might apply for — this may have an impact on the number of courses you choose to take. In addition, student loans are usually only available if you are a full-time student. Check with the Student Loans Office at your university/college to see if your planned course load fulfills their requirements. (Some student loans are now being made available to part-time students, and those in shorter programs. Again, check your school for specifics.)

You might also remember that you don't have to take every course you're interested in while you are at university full-time. An Angus Reid survey of employees, conducted in 1997 for the Royal Bank of Canada, found that 50% of survey respondents took at least one course that year to upgrade work knowledge and skills. The same percentage plans to do so again next year. "In order to keep current, they have to continuously upgrade their skills and level of knowledge...extra training and education is one of the components that allows people to deal with the degree of change and have higher job satisfaction." (Bruce Cameron, Senior Vice President, Angus Reid Group) Learning is a lifelong process. Design a program that works well for you now, and know that you have plenty of time to study all that interests you later.

Step 2: Which Courses are for You?

What courses should I take? That depends on where you are in your career-planning process. The more clarity you have about your career direction, the easier it is to choose your courses. If you already know what program you are planning to follow, then the university calendar should describe your program requirements fairly specifically. Try to take the prerequisites first, because they are the door openers to higher level courses. Some programs have specific core courses and then offer you the opportunity to select options or electives to make up the required number of credits toward your degree. (If you have trouble with these terms, consult the "Know Your Terms" section earlier in this book.)

Other programs are open-ended and you have more freedom to choose. Usually you will need to select your faculty (Arts, Science, Management, Engineering, Education, and so on). You may need to fulfill certain requirements in terms of types of courses (perhaps Arts or Sciences), or you may have to declare a major area of specialization (such as political science or biology). Each university and college has its own pattern of programming, so it is essential that you use the calendar to plan.

Some universities, such as the University of Calgary, offer a first year of General Studies. This allows you to postpone the choice of a faculty and a major, while you take a selection of courses and explore possibilities. You may discover that although you really enjoy conversational Spanish, you are not excited by the academic aspects of Spanish literature. (This might eliminate Spanish as a Major.) At the same time, you may have discovered the possibilities of Microbiology, and be eager to explore career options in that field. A note of caution, however: a general studies year does not always solve your career dilemma. You may want to be more proactive and undertake specific career planning, rather than simply opting for General Studies.

The best advice we can give you is to get good advice! There are as many different patterns of course selection as there are programs of study. Plan to consult two specific resources: the calendar (see the tips below), and your faculty's academic advisors. Academic advisors are the people who can ensure that you are interpreting the calendar correctly, and that you are planning for the right mix of courses to progress in your program. New, first-year students can usually access an advisor during orientation week, and sometimes during the summer months prior to fall registration. Consult with someone as early as possible — and preferably before registration — so you will know you are on the right track from the beginning.

Some Tips on Using the Calendar for Course Selection:
Every calendar has a section for each faculty in the institution. The faculties are usually listed alphabetically. Each faculty's course offerings are described in the relevant section.

- All courses offered are listed in the calendar. Courses are identified by letter and number codes, and the coding system is unique to each institution. The letter usually refers to the course subject (e.g. Econ for Economics) and the number refers to the course level (e.g. first year courses numbered 101).

onsultants

Choosing courses can be stressful! Here are some tips:

- *Remind yourself of your client's interests and skills.*
- *Help your client to review her goals, however tentative.*
- *Encourage him to select a variety of courses which he will find enticing.*
- *Support her in her choices.*
- *Remind yourself that no choices are final.*
- *Encourage him to select courses which will keep his options open, until he has decided on a firm career direction.*

Almost all schools now have either phone-in registration or computer-assisted registration. The instructions on "how to" will be clearly explained in your calendar. Most schools also offer electronic access to help you to check on the availability of courses.

- Check to see if you need a prerequisite before you can enroll (e.g. Math 101 to enroll in Business Statistics).

- Check to see if the course (or specific sections of that course) are open, or are reserved for a special group (e.g. first year teaching students). Note when the course is being offered: fall, winter, spring, or all.

- Choose to complete your program prerequisites first. They are door-openers and good over-view courses — they will give you a sample of what may come next.

- Read the graduation requirements. You will need a minimum number of courses and credits, at various levels, to graduate. Some colleges and universities also stipulate certain required combinations (such as Sciences and Arts) before they will grant you a degree.

- If you have trouble getting into a course because it is full, talk to your advisor to see whether anything can be done, or try to add the course during the first week of classes once other students may have dropped out.

- If your first choice course is full, register in something else in case spaces do not become available. At least you'll have the number of courses you need.

Thoughts on Choosing an Instructor/ Professor:
You will not always have a choice of professors, but if you do, a little research can go a long way. Some Student Councils publish a book that rates professors based on student evaluations. They report on how well professors prepare for their classes, and whether they are well-organized, interesting, knowledgeable, current, offering useful hand-outs, setting fair exams, and so on. Or you can ask other students who have taken a class from the professor you are investigating — just beware of personal biases or personality conflicts that might skew the feedback you receive. If you have an opportunity, the best method of evaluation is probably to sit in on a class and observe the professor in action!

Once you get into a class, you may want out:
Once the term begins, you may find you have more courses than you can handle, or that you intensely dislike one of them and want to withdraw. Most universities have clear-cut policies for withdrawing from courses and programs. Usually, you can drop and add courses without penalty within the first week of classes. After that you can still withdraw, until about two-thirds of the way through the semester, and avoid failing. Your withdrawal will be noted on your record, however, and you are only permitted a limited number of withdrawals on your record at graduation. You also won't get your money back for the course unless you withdraw during that first "drop/add week."

Transferring from College to University:
A Note on Course Selection
If you are a college student, and you plan to continue your education by completing a degree at university, you can usually transfer from college to university after one semester, two semesters (one year), or after two years.

Wherever possible, choose "university transfer" courses while you are at college. Each university has its own criteria for accepting courses from other institutions; one university may turn down a course that another will accept. Usually, the choice is based on how closely the course content and level of difficulty compare with similar courses at that university. When you choose courses for transfer, try to select those that are most likely to be accepted by a number of universities, so you can keep your options open. Also check with universities directly to ensure that they will recognize each course you want to transfer. You can expect that basic, first-year overview courses are more generally accepted for transfer, as there is less variation in the level of difficulty or course content.

Some universities stipulate core courses that you must have taken at college before you can declare a major or enter a faculty at university. For example, some Management faculties require that you have at least some basic courses in Economics, Accounting and Math. Again, check the calendar.

Hints

When checking with universities about accepting a course for transfer:
• *Contact the relevant department and ask for the subject advisor.*
• *Give the course name and code, e.g. Introduction to Psychology, Psyc 205.*
• *Be prepared to submit the course outline from the calendar, or include the course outline that your professor provided at the beginning of the term.*
• *Include the author, title and publication date of the textbook assigned.*

Step 3: Plan to Be There!

At university, you are pretty much on your own. No one is responsible to check up on you, or to see that you are performing. This is a big switch from high school, or from the working world. In high school, your progress is tracked — you are in class every day, you have regular homework assignments to complete, if you don't show up someone will know and you can expect consequences. In the workplace, your supervisor monitors your work, demands regular attendance and certain standards, and again if you don't show up someone will impose consequences.

University life is different. Here you are required to discipline yourself to a far greater extent. Your professor will not notice if you are missing when he or she is speaking to a sea of 300 faces. Similarly, if you do not attend the tutorials, your Teaching Assistant will assume that you have made the choice to stay away, and that it is your business. The temptation, of course, is to think it doesn't matter if no one is watching. You can learn what you need to from books, or from someone else's notes. That's denial. It's an enticing thought, but it's not true. Inevitably, if you choose not to show up, there will be consequences.

First of all, in many tutorials, language and science labs — and occasionally in lectures — someone does take attendance. Sometimes your attendance counts for a percentage of your final grade (marks that are pretty easy to earn if you simply show up prepared). Instructors remember your attendance or absence when they start marking exams and essays, and the interest or lack of interest you have shown will influence the mark you receive.

Furthermore, instructors like to spring occasional in-class tests — to entice people to show up and keep up. If you are absent and cannot prove that you had a good reason for being absent (illness, a death in the family, your car really did break down and you can produce the mechanic's bill), you can definitely forget about those marks.

Tutorials and labs are opportunities to practice — your ideas, your ability to discuss, your skill at applying concepts, using tools, and generating results. Consistently missing these classes is throwing away your practice time. You will usually end up having to work harder for less result.

Be pragmatic! The topics covered in tutorials and lectures frequently appear on exams almost exactly as they were taught during the year. There is often a definite point of view or a precise style of thinking which the instructor is looking for in the answer. You may say that's not fair, or you may question whether that's learning, but it is still true. You cannot depend solely on your study of the course textbooks to succeed on exams. It's not all there.

The bottom line?
There is a strong positive correlation between
regular attendance and high marks.
Be Smart and Be There!

Step 4: Making Time for Everything Else

Course selection and time for academics is only the beginning. Most campuses offer a wide range of opportunities for you to become involved in other activities. Check out the various clubs, societies and social opportunities that might appeal to you. Know that the choice may be overwhelming, and that you may be tempted to sign up for too many activities. Take a good look at your committed time (classes, part-time work, homework, volunteering) and then sign up for one or two extracurricular activities that will add to the quality of your life on campus without overburdening you with time commitments, additional costs, or any other stressors. This is a great time to stretch in many directions — as long as you don't take it past the breaking point!

Two types of activities bear special mention: athletics and volunteering...

Some Thoughts About Athletics:
You may have planned to attend university or college specifically to participate in an athletics program.

Real Life

Leah slept in most mornings, and usually missed her first two classes. For a while, a few classmates would lend Leah their notes — her stories for missing class were generally somewhat plausible. After a few weeks, though, she started getting the cold shoulder. Her fellow students refused to share their notes, she got further behind, the situation began to feel desperate. Mid-term exams were a disaster, and she lost participation marks for not attending her tutorials. Dropping out started to feel like an option. After a frank talk with her T.A., Leah made a decision to show up in class and become an active learner. She had a lot of catching up to do, but dropping out would have cost her a student loan, and some dignity.

Consider exactly what you hope to become involved in: are you preparing to become a professional athlete, trying out for a spot on a university team, or do you want to play a sport for fun and recreation? Your athletic goals will dictate the time and energy commitments you need to make, and the consequences.

If athletics is to become your major focus, know that you still need to maintain a full academic course load (4 to 5 courses a semester) and keep your grades at a certain acceptable level. It is unlikely that most of your professors will condone missed tests and late or incomplete assignments. Their first priority, as you might expect, is academics. Similarly, your coach or athletic director will not normally accept academic deadlines as a reasonable excuse for missing practice or a game. Athletes travel frequently during the semester, spend hours on buses and endure cramped quarters. They must be extremely adept at managing time and balancing competing demands. Know what you are in for!

Arlin volunteered at a centre for brain injury rehabilitation, where he impressed people with his skills and dedication. As a result, he was offered summer work at the centre, an experience that helped him choose his career direction. The director of the centre gave him an excellent reference when he applied (and was accepted) to a doctoral program in Neuropsychology. Through his volunteer experience, Arlin met influential people, learned more about his interests and skills, found a career direction and opened doors to future employment.

If recreational athletics is what appeals to you, check out your campus Recreation Centre and join up for the sports of your choice, on a regular or drop-in basis. The secret in this case is to make athletics fit with the rest of your schedule, so that you feel in control and enjoy the exercise and camaraderie.

A Note On Volunteering:
Volunteering may seem like a strange topic to raise at the end of discussions on financial and academic pressures. Clearly, you are going to have a lot on your plate already. But there are some important advantages to saving a bit of time for volunteer commitments, which we encourage you to think about here...

Many professional programs, including social work, education, medicine, speech language pathology and others, expect student applicants to have previous or current volunteer experience in their chosen field of study. In fact, volunteering is often one of the major selection criteria for entry into a program. As you work and study to prepare yourself for entry into a professional program, you need to plan for some volunteer time.

One of the reasons universities emphasize volunteerism is that it demonstrates your willingness to contribute time and energy to the community, and to activities that "make a difference." Volunteerism is a sign of a well-rounded character, capable of responsibility and generosity, as well as good grades and athletic accomplishment. You will also learn new skills as a volunteer. These may stand you in good stead when you are doing a practicum, or when you need to draw on practical experience to answer an exam question or plan an assignment.

Another reason universities use volunteerism as a selection criterion is that they want you to have researched and thought about your choice of career. You are then less likely to drop out halfway through the program. Dropping out is extremely costly to the university and to you. Volunteering is also an excellent opportunity to explore career options. You can experience an occupation (or at least an occupational environment) from the inside, without a long-term investment in preparation and study. You get the "inside scoop" before you commit yourself to a program.

Several of the most generous scholarships available are awarded to students who have contributed actively to their communities. Many other scholarships and financial awards use volunteering as one of their selection criteria.

Finally, one of the rewards of volunteering is the network of people you develop: people who can support you, introduce you to others, open doors, or perhaps ultimately offer you a job. Volunteering to contribute in your community is a pragmatic and practical (as well as generous) use of your time.

All work and no play???
Finding a balance between school, work, and your personal and social life is important. It is also easier said than done. The trick is to be adaptable, and to respond to your own circumstances. You are accountable to yourself: if you party too hard and let your grades slide, you pay the penalty. If you keep your head in your books and never surface for fun, you miss out on friendships and social contact, and you burn yourself out needlessly. Learning to balance work and play is a challenge — and it probably always will be — as your needs grow and change.

R eal Life

As a recent graduate and a current job hunter, Paul is thankful for his volunteer participation in clubs at school. Employers seem to be far more interested in what he did with his time, than whether he got an A or a B. Many employers don't even ask for mark transcripts during a job interview, but all have asked what activities Paul participated in at university. It's more constructive, Paul has found, to earn a B/B+ average and "have a life" than to work 24 hours a day, seven days a week to earn straight A's.

H ints

Canada Trust offers generous scholarships to students with outstanding records of contributing to their communities – students who volunteer and make a difference.

You're leaving home! Joy! Freedom! Apartment-hunting! If you attend university or college away from your home town (or if living with your parents is just not an option), you will have to find a place to live and perhaps someone (or more than one) to live with. This is your next challenge; again our goal is to help you make an informed decision.

The application packages universities send you will usually contain information on accommodation. Most universities offer some sort of student housing — residences or dormitories ranging from large, utilitarian structures full of small single or shared rooms to self-contained apartments and townhouses. Usually, universities will also have a housing referral service, or at least bulletin boards where people advertise available accommodation.

Your choices are many, varied, and more or less appealing. You'll need to consider your budget, your personality, your personal needs, and the availability of options. Essentially, you have these possibilities: residence on campus, or off-campus (alone or shared) housing. Here is our review of your basic options:

1. On-Campus Residences. Many students recommend living in residence for your first year (and perhaps beyond that). Most residences offer shared accommodation; some single rooms may be available. Check for floors with co-ed or same sex options, as well as those known for "partying" or "studying."

2. Renting a room in a family home. Some families will include you as a family member. One student we know was treated like the "prodigal son." He lived with a couple whose own family had grown and left home. They made his meals, did his laundry, cleaned his room and packed his lunches. (This is very unusual.) More often you will rent a room or a basement suite, probably make your own meals, and take care of your own needs. The room is usually furnished, but every situation will be different, so take a close look. You may arrange to shovel snow and cut grass, in return for meals or a rent reduction.

ON-CAMPUS RESIDENCES

Advantages	Disadvantages
• On campus • Close to classes • Saves time and transportation • College spirit • Meal plans available • Less responsibility for homemaking • Safer, especially if you are new in city/town • Co-ed floors and same-sex floors • First step in leaving home • Meet lots of people, and make friends	• Cramped living space • Shared rooms • Noisy • Grades can suffer from lack of sleep • Institutional • Lack of privacy • May dislike your roommate

RENTING A ROOM IN A FAMILY HOME

Advantages	Disadvantages
• Off campus — walking distance • Quiet • Private • Independent • May have meals provided • Or, be self-sufficient • Possibly, some family support	• Off campus — requiring transportation • Lonely • Perhaps unintentionally involved in domestic issues • Lack of privacy • Difficult house rules • Restriction on visitors • Poor cooking facilities

3. Sharing a house or apartment. This is a favourite choice for many students. The choice of apartment or house will make a difference — you may find yourself considering them both, at different times, during your university years. Sharing an apartment usually involves only one, or perhaps two, roommates. A house often includes more people. Usually, the space is unfurnished. Both options have advantages and disadvantages.

4. Living alone. This option is the most autonomous. You make decisions that affect only you. It will probably be more expensive, and it may also be isolating. However, if your budget allows, it may also be the right option for you.

Obviously, your first choice of accommodation may not be your last. Needs and circumstances change. What worked in your first year may be inappropriate in your second year. You may lose or add roommates. Always remember that you do have choices, and that you can change your mind or make a different decision if needed. (Most property managers, however, expect you to sign a lease. Check the conditions and see if you can live with them.)

Whatever configuration you choose, a common concern is what to do about your accommodation if you go home for the summer. Again, there are options. You can give up your place and find another one in the fall. In that case you will have to store your stuff (or take it home), and you will have to find a new place when everyone else is scrambling to find one, too. On the other hand, you save four months' rent. Or you could decide to keep your place, continue to pay the rent and stay at home rent-free for the summer. You might be able to sublet your home to an out-of-town summer student who needs accommodation for a few months (check your lease for rules on subletting, and discuss it with your landlord/lady). Or one of your roommates may stay on during the summer, to attend summer school or to work. In that case, you would pay your share of the costs and know that you had a place to come back to in the fall.

C

SHARING A HOUSE OR APARTMENT

Advantages

- Off campus-walking distance
- Independence
- Can live with friends
- Can choose lifestyle
- Freedom to have company
- Can cook own meals
- Cheaper if rent and utilities shared
- Usually someone to talk to
- Can have pets (maybe)
- Can develop house rules to live by

Disadvantages

- Off campus... requires transportation
- Lease may be restricting
- Possible roommate problems
- Issues with 'moochers' who stay, eat your food and don't contribute
- Issues around sharing costs, food, space
- Who is responsible for lease, utilities, rent, phone?
- Their friends are not your friends
- Lack of privacy
- Noisy
- Pets cause problems
- House rules become burdensome or are rejected
- Someone (or more than one) may leave you stuck with unpaid bills or increased expenses
- Rarely conducive to studying, because of different schedules; study more at library and school

LIVING ALONE

Advantages

- Autonomy and freedom to make decisions
- Live your own lifestyle
- Cook your own meals
- Come and go as you choose
- Freedom to have company
- Quiet, conducive to studying

Disadvantages

- Lonely
- Expensive
- Isolated

The Big Challenge: Choosing a Roommate

"Roommates" sounds fun, festive, and easygoing — friends for life, right? Not so fast! It really isn't quite that easy. The students we talked to offered one unanimous piece of advice — based on experience, experimentation and living with the outcome. ***Don't choose your best, or closest, or even less close friend as your roommate!***

"Why not? (you say) We get along so well together. We share everything..."

Well, that's precisely why! At home, your friends go back to their places after you've been together. You have separate spaces, separate identities, separate lives. The best way for many of you to lose your friends is to room with them. Rooming with close friends can bring out the worst in all of us. Those annoying habits that you can tolerate or ignore for a few hours become motives for murder when you can't escape them. Those things you always took for granted in your friends may become contentious: borrowing clothes, books, personal items. Their behaviours, their choices, their other friends — to say nothing of their attitudes toward chores, money, studying and student life — may drive you crazy. Even if you knew all these things about them before, you didn't have to live with them.

Okay, we know some of you will decide to live with friends anyway. So we suggest you read the following section carefully. It might save your friendship!

How *do* you find a roommate? Again, here are some suggestions from experienced students...

- If you are living in a university residence, you may not have a choice. In that case you will find that you learn skills for getting along — or you appeal to the Residence Office for a change if things aren't going well.

- You may know someone from home who is willing to share your cramped dorm room. Be prepared to negotiate do's and don'ts, boundaries, and personal space (more on this later).

- If you don't know anyone, and you want to share an apartment, the university Accommodation Liaison person may have a list of students also looking to share.

The big consideration is compatibility. So how do you know if you're compatible? First, be brutally honest about you! Sit down with a blank sheet of paper and describe yourself: likes (clean clothes, ice cream for breakfast, perfect calm), dislikes (squeaky floors, dirty socks, Motown). Write down everything you can think of, insignificant or otherwise, and then mark the most important items. Now, just for fun, see if you can write an "ad" about yourself, one that you might read in a "companions wanted" column of the newspaper. Give an honest thumbnail sketch, including as many useful details as you can. You are not only choosing a roommate, you are also becoming a roommate.

Now, write down the traits and characteristics you would look for in a roommate, so that you could get along relatively well, and would have enough in common not to grate on each other. Ask yourself what is most important, and what you can live with if you have to. You may be allergic to cigarette smoke and cat hair, be a vegetarian and a morning person, and have a preference for Gregorian Chant. Someone out there is a late riser, brings home stray animals, smokes his lungs out and craves Heavy Metal. Not a great idea.

What about gender? Some students prefer to have same-sex roommates; others get on better with a roomie of the opposite sex. In some arrangements, you may have several men and women living compatibly together. The decision will depend on your own preferences.

If possible, talk to potential candidates by phone or e-mail. Better still, arrange a meeting if you are not too far away. Share your profile with your prospective roommate, and ask them lots of questions about themselves. It really is important to know as much as you can about their habits, preferences, attitudes, values and beliefs.

Real Life

Chad was going away to graduate school. He phoned his new university to ask for a list of students who were also looking for roommates. He was given several names that appeared to be 'good fits.' After conducting long distance telephone interviews with each of them, he chose Paul. They spent more time getting to know each other by 'chatting' on e-mail. They agreed to meet, talk, and then look for a place together. Their shared accommodation worked well for the first year. After that, they both made other plans.

You may choose to answer an ad for a group of roommates who are looking for one more. In this case, be sure you:

- Meet everyone living in the house;
- Find out about chores (you may get the worst ones as the new person), meals, friends dropping in or staying over, whether cliques have already formed, how the rent is paid, telephone rules;
- Think about all the other considerations we have discussed!

The Next Big Challenge: Finding a Place

Once you have identified a roommate, the next step is to find a place (unless the roommate comes equipped with premises). Decide in advance what you can afford, remembering to include rent, damage deposits, utilities, cable, and telephone. Do you each need your own phone line (costing more, but eliminating conflict over time or long distance charges)? Do you need additional lines for computers?

When the search is over and you have found a spot, we strongly suggest you both sign the lease. Demonstrate that you are equally responsible and accountable. Recognize that if you decide to part, you will need to negotiate who leaves and who stays. All this sounds very businesslike because it is meant to! You will spend a lot of money on your home away from home. Some students move in with the first available roommate and what follows isn't pretty: several more moves per semester, unpaid bills, extra live-ins, or a home that resembles a garbage dump!

Before you sign your lease — indeed before you agree to share accommodation — discuss and negotiate your important agreements for shared living. (Use the list below to guide your discussion.) If you can't agree on these ahead of time, you both need to look for someone else!

C

Agreements For Shared Living

- Who is responsible for the rent, utilities, phone, and cable payments? We suggest both or all share the responsibility for signing the lease and making the monthly payments. Consider paying an extra installment of your month's rent and utilities into a trust fund, so that if someone leaves without notice you are covered for a month while you find a new roomie.

- Assigning cupboard and fridge space in the kitchen gives each of you some control. Often, roomies cook or prepare their food independently, allowing for different schedules. Keeping supplies separated reduces argument potential.

- Negotiating rooms so that the amount of private space is relatively equal can be a challenge. Make good trades, for example the person with the smaller room gets the covered parking space, or the extra closet, or the smaller rent share.

- Respecting each person's space and privacy is important. This includes a willingness to listen to your music through headphones, reducing or eliminating visitors during study times, knocking on a closed door before entering.

- Discuss frankly how you will manage friends (including boy/girl friends) staying overnight or visiting from out-of-town. Decide what is acceptable and manageable to you. This should include people who crash for a night and then stay for a month or a term, because they were evicted from somewhere else. This is a big issue for many students, because it can so easily discount everything you agreed on earlier! Be flexible, but don't agree under pressure to a situation that may cause stress later. (The same goes for keeping pets!)

- Clarify your standards and expectations around cleanliness. You may want to split the chores in the common areas (living room, kitchen, bathroom, hall way), and take responsibility for your own room. No one else will clean up your mess. Do your own

Real Life

Jan had an apartment, but hated living alone. Her first roommate was a girlfriend she knew from high school. Cheri worked full-time, so she had evenings free to rent movies and have friends over. This soon became a problem for Jan, who needed quiet study time at night and on weekends, and hated having to ask Cheri and her friends to keep the noise down. After one particularly noisy evening, and a kitchen full of dirty dishes, Jan asked Cheri to leave.

Jan's next roommate was Brad. "At least he won't leave his mess all over the bathroom, and he's a student too, so he'll understand about 'quiet.'" Brad was quiet — so quiet and invisible that Jan wanted to scream! Brad left after one semester, because he thought Jan was too noisy and left too much of her stuff in the bathroom!

dishes. This is a big issue for roomies. Most people don't like cleaning, or haven't had to do their own. However, no one ever died from cleaning a toilet — and some people almost die when they have to use a filthy one!

- If you don't do your share, your roommate(s) may make life miserable for you until you pull your weight. A student told us of a situation where one roommate neglected to do the dishes when it was his turn. The dishes piled up for days; eventually there were no clean ones left. His roommates started eating out and handing their meal receipts to the culprit who let his chores slide. He not only had to foot the hefty take-out food bills, he also had to clean up the accumulated mess and tolerate the humiliation!

- Keep the communication lines open. You will disagree from time to time, or you will become irritated or annoyed. Talk about your concerns. Resolve your differences. If you keep quiet, they won't go away — instead they will escalate and potentially destroy a good relationship.

Finally, Some Thoughts About Living At Home:
If you have the option, you may choose to live at home while you pursue your education. If you do, perhaps nothing about living at home will change. But the odds are that your parents will expect some modifications, and so will you. In some ways, your relationship will be different. You are more independent, and more accountable. You will probably expect to be treated like an adult. Your parents may be quite prepared to rise to the occasion. However, that usually happens only if you are both willing to talk about your expectations.

As an adult living at home, you may be expected to share some of the responsibilities for the mechanics of living. Perhaps you contribute your share of the household chores (cooking, cleaning, or shopping for groceries) in return for the privilege of living at home and using the resources that home provides. In turn, you might expect that your parents no longer check your comings and goings, comment on the hours you keep, or share their opinions of the friends you choose.

Fundamentally, we suggest, respect one another's privacy. Respect that you are adults and you are humans. Make allowances for one another as you grow into a new relationship. Above all, talk to each other about what works and what doesn't, and experiment with new alternatives.

The Hard Truth About Workload

Carl breezed through high school with good grades. University was his first taste of freedom. He played hard, slept late, did his essays on the run. His grades started to slip. He pulled 'all-nighters' before exams, showing up bleary-eyed and exhausted. That had always worked for him in high school. It didn't work now. The Dean wrote him a warning letter, which he ignored. At Christmas, he received a polite invitation from the Dean to withdraw from the program and the university, because his GPA was considered too low. To put it bluntly, he failed his semester.

Fact Number One: The workload — in university and in other post-secondary institutions — is heavy. Don't be lulled into a false sense of security just because your schedule shows fewer classroom hours than you had in high school. For every hour you spend in classroom lectures or tutorials, you will need an additional three hours for homework, readings, assignments and studying. That adds up:

5 courses @ 3 class hours per week
= 15 hours in class
and
15 class hours @ 3 homework hours each
= 45 hours homework
for a total of
15 + 45 = 60 hours per week

Fact Number Two: If you do not keep up with the work on a weekly basis, you will create brutal stress for yourself. To the great frustration of students, essays and exams are scheduled for about the same time in most courses. If you take five courses and leave all the work to the same three weekends in November or March, you set yourself up to fail (to say nothing of the fact that it is incredibly difficult to actually learn anything that way).

Of course, you manage your workload to some extent by the number and type of courses you select each semester. Beyond that, however, the key lies in smart studying. Our purpose here is to equip you to make the most of every hour you spend on your studies — whether that is an hour in the classroom, at the library, or at your desk at home. *The single best way to buy time for all the things you want to do, and still achieve the academic results you need, is to study smart.*

Our Top Four Study Smart Strategies — VIS.1 (very important section number one)

Step 1: Get It Right From the Start: Focus in Class

- Arrive in time to get a good seat — you want to see and hear the professor clearly.
- Screen out what's unimportant — listen carefully for tone of voice, emphasis, repetition, and hints.
- Be a critical thinker — discern the difference between fact and opinion, and be conscious of your instructor's bias.
- Be a smart, strategic, creative note-taker...

What's the big deal about good notes? Three things. First, you are going to forget half of what was said within a few days of the lecture; 80% will be gone within a month. Second, most instructors base their exam questions on what they said in class. One plus two equals three: if you plan to do well, then efficient, accurate, integrated notes are essential.

So how do you take good notes?

1. Listen for the main ideas or themes of the lecture, and the main supporting evidence. This is smarter than trying to write down every word.

2. Use abbreviations... use sub-headings... and underline or highlight important words and definitions. Be creative. Illustrate the most important points quickly.

3. Use loose-leaf paper and a binder, rather than a "scribbler." Add reading notes and class hand-outs in the appropriate spots. Write on only one side of your paper. (The other side is then available for textbook notes and after-thoughts.)

4. Leave a reasonable margin on every page so you can add key or summary words alongside.

5. Practice Mind-Mapping. Once you learn it, this is a great technique for taking notes in class, studying for tests and exams, and planning/developing themes for a project or essay. (See below for further details.)

Real Life

Tracey left most things to the last minute. "That's the way I am," she explained. "I need to wait until the last minute to get going." Before she knew it, she had three assignments due in the same week, as well as a mid-term exam. In a panic, she asked two of her professors for extensions, so that she could complete one essay and study for the mid-terms. One professor reluctantly gave her a 24-hour extension, which was not very helpful. The other asked, "Why do you consider my course less important than your others?" He refused her the extra time, and suggested she get herself organized!

6. Consider using your computer in class. Some universities are now wired for NotePads in the classroom, either at the graduate level or throughout the university (Acadia University, Ecole des Hautes Etudes Commercials, affiliated with the University of Montreal, and Queen's University are examples), and professors are beginning to use these tools in innovative ways. Most universities and colleges will soon follow suit. This will change the way students learn in the classroom, as well as how you study at home.

Step 2: Pick your time and place — there's nothing like concentration

• Choose study times when you can concentrate without distraction. (If your roommate is partying, or your baby sister is screaming, or you feel so guilty about not having done the dishes, perhaps there's a better time — or a better place...)

• Work in a quiet, well-lit area where you can spread out all the books and papers you need. Your concentration will improve if you study in the same pleasant, comfortable place each day. (Kitchens are usually distracting, as is any place where other people come and go.) Make space for papers and books as well as the computer.

• Some research suggests that relaxing music assists your capacity to learn. Studies show that slow (adagio) movements, particularly by Baroque composers like Vivaldi, are excellent. Loud music with lyrics and a heavy beat is often distracting. Experiment to see what works for you. You may actually prefer the quiet.

• Follow a regular study schedule to get more done. All life operates in rhythms. If you are tired or hungry, you will remember less, and of course the process will be more painful. "Early to bed and early to rise" is actually good advice. You probably can't change the fact that you will remember more when you study after a good night's sleep. (If you are not a morning person by inclination, you can work on training yourself to a new rhythm.) Most people don't study well in the early afternoon. Try exercising then instead!

- Sleeping until noon, however tempting, costs you a lot of valuable brain time. If you are not a morning person, schedule morning classes so that you are forced to get up earlier. (This will take some getting used to, and you may be tempted to sleep in and skip class. Persist!) Remember, your grades are on the line, and you have significant money invested in your success.

- Start your study session with a course that you are interested in, and work for about 50 minutes. Then take a 10-minute break — have a glass of cold water, stretch, and take some deep breaths outside. Study a further 50 minutes and take a second break. You will get further, and remember more, if you "chunk" your time and materials in this way. Some students study their least-favourite courses first, to get them out of the way. Experiment with what works for you. (One thing is for sure — if you use your time efficiently, you'll have more time left over for fun.)

Post these reminders near your computer, in the front of a notebook, or on the back of your hand...

Limit your distractions.
Find good space.
Try classical music.
Create a daily schedule.
Sleep in between semesters.
Use the 50/10 study session plan.

Step 3: Learn How to Read!

Don't read your textbooks like you would your favourite novel. (Undoubtedly we do not need to tell you this. Most students do not confuse the two.) Read textbooks with purpose, if not always passion...

Read Effectively— by reading with concentration and intent. • Find the author's major ideas, rather than getting caught in the minor details. • Skim over a section before you take notes, then take notes only on what you need. • Use your dictionary well. (Look up all the words you don't know and make a point of using them in another situation within 24 hours — watch your vocabulary grow!)

Real Life

Graeme seemed to have less homework than the other students in his class, even though he was taking a full load of sciences. He told us his secret: he listened carefully in class, he asked questions, and he took great notes. He was focused and attentive. In his words, "if I'm going to be there anyway, I might as well use the time profitably." Frequently, he completed much of the assigned homework by the time class was over. Working smart — rather than hard — gave him the opportunity to do well, and pursue his other interests.

Hints

Drink lots of water. Water hydrates your brain. It balances the electrolytes. It provides a medium for electrical currents. It tastes cool!

Read Selectively— which is not the same as speed reading. Reading selectively is skimming the material for that which is relevant. • Preview each chapter. Check the introduction for a sense of subject matter. • Skim the body for content — proofs, examples, ideas, calculations. • Use the conclusion to revisit key points and test your comprehension. • Writers often use trigger words alerting you to the most important points. Watch for phrases such as "what is important," "an illustration," "for example," and "this is crucial." Words and phrases such as "on the other hand," "in addition," and "however," are further clues to the writer's intent.

Remember, though, this is not a substitute for thorough reading! Some material should be read selectively, and some needs to be read thoroughly. This will depend on how complex the material is, how well it is covered in class, how central the ideas are to the course, how the author writes, and how important the topic is to you.

Read Critically— One of the most important mindsets you can develop in university is the tendency to question what you read. • Learn to discern the importance of information, and to spot the difference between fact and opinion.• Observe author biases and evaluate the relevance and timeliness of ideas. • Use critical reading in all your courses. Not everything (in fact, very little) that is written is the final truth. Facts can frequently be disputed — and replaced by somebody elses.

Read Actively— Read a section first and then make notes. Use a highlighter selectively, on keywords and phrases only (you don't want to read the whole thing again at exam time).• Make notes about your questions, comments and concerns. • Integrate your lecture notes with your reading notes.• Notice differences of opinion between the text book authors and your professor. Such differences make good questions in your next class or tutorial!

If you don't read effectively, you won't understand the information, or be able to use it in your essays, exams or assignments. Reading a wide range of material increases your vocabulary. Increasing your vocabulary improves your communication, and allows you to express your ideas more convincingly. Communication is the single most important transferable skill, at school and in the world of work.

Step 4: As with anything, there's no substitute for practice...

- Review your notes once a week — to keep the material familiar, and to spot the patterns of thought which are developing.
- Stick to your study schedule.
- Use 'flash cards' for memorizing facts, dates, definitions, formulae, and new vocabulary.

Any performance coach — in athletics or music, for example — will use time-saving, skill-building drills and techniques to develop excellence. So it is with us as study coaches...

A) Try SQ3R (and survey/question/read/recite/review)

First, survey your materials with a quick read. Second (based on what you have read), create some questions you will be able to answer once you have mastered the content. Third, go back through the materials again, chunking your information by reading a paragraph, reciting it back in your own words, and reviewing what you have learned. Fourth, return to answer the questions you created at the beginning of the exercise. Finally, check your answers and make any necessary corrections. (Some textbooks provide study questions at the back of each chapter; these may work well with this technique.)

B) Build PRWR (to preview/read/write/recite)

Preview the chapter, article, or whatever you are studying, to become generally familiar with the information, and to make a note of the important points. Now read a section carefully. Follow this by writing notes in your own words about the materials you have read. Check that you have covered all the important points in the section. Finally, recite back to yourself what you have written. Continue this process until you are confident you have mastered the information.

C) The Best, Most Creative Technique: Mind Mapping

Mind Mapping assumes that we do not necessarily think in straight lines, from left to right and top to bottom. Rather, we also think in clusters, patterns, themes, and perhaps pictures. Mind Mapping allows you to establish themes and sub-themes, and then to cluster the main, important concepts together as they occur to you, or as you study the material.

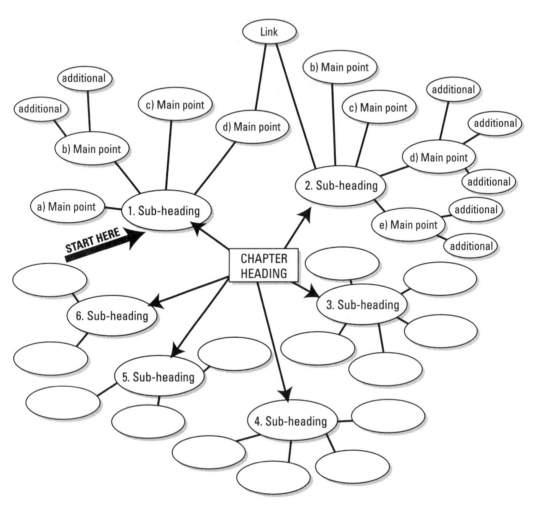

Here is an example of Mind Mapping for organizing notes from a text book: add sub-headings clockwise from "10 o'clock"

If you were to translate this particular mind map back into traditional note-taking (working clockwise from "10 o'clock"), you would get this:

Chapter Heading:
1. Sub-heading
      a) Main point
      b) Main point
            (i)   additional
            (ii)   additional
      c) Main point
      d) Main point

2. Sub-heading
      a) Main point (see connection with 1d above)
      b) Main point
      c) Main point
      d) Main point
            (i)   additional
            (ii)   additional
            (ii)   additional
      e) Main point
            (i)   additional
            (ii)   additional

and so on...

Advantages of Mind Mapping

- The Mind Map allows you to "see" the whole picture almost at a glance. The traditional note-taking structure requires you to follow lines down and across in sequence.

- The Mind Map is flexible — you can add ideas or information as you go.

- You can often record all the information you need on one page using a Mind Map. Rarely can you condense traditional note taking onto a single page.

- Mind Maps encourage you to use main points and few words to capture an idea. Traditional note taking often becomes a wordy or verbatim commentary.

Disadvantages of Mind Mapping

- You will likely have to re-think note taking.

- You will need practice to use this technique effectively.

- Other students may have difficulty using your notes, if you share.

MIND MAP EXAMPLE I

ENGLISH

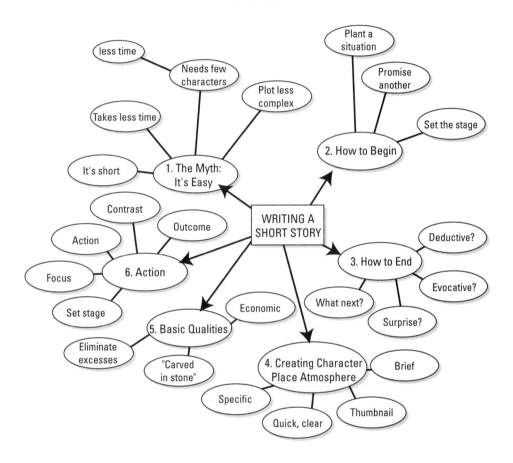

MIND MAP EXAMPLE II

COMMUNICATION

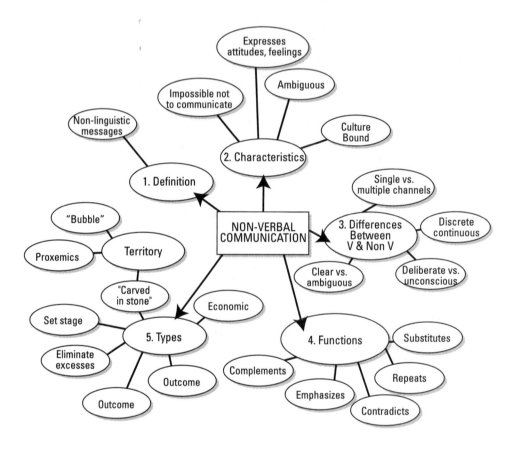

MIND MAP EXAMPLE III

BUSINESS MANAGEMENT

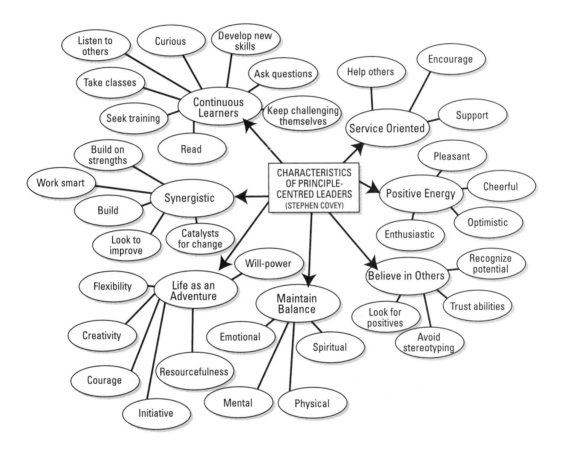

A Note on University Study Skills Resources...

(Most universities offer at least some of the following...) *Study skills workshops* can help you become an effective student by teaching you how to organize your time, take good notes, and manage your workload.

Writing labs offer you the opportunity to learn the basics of assignment-writing, using accepted academic formats and appropriate referencing. Some labs will also review essential writing skills such as grammar and punctuation.

Library tours will introduce you to library facilities and information retrieval systems — including the Internet. Familiarity with these systems will enhance your research, writing, and study skills.

Special tutorials are usually offered to assist students in any subject area, particularly math, sciences and economics. These tutorials are often run by teaching assistants and may help build your understanding of the basics. They do not usually count for grades. Participate in these tutorials early in the semester, before you run into trouble. The strategies you learn will give you a head start and build the confidence you need to do well.

Resource Centres sometimes offer one-on-one tutoring. You will be paired with a senior student who has experience and interest in a field where you need help. This may or may not be offered on a fee-for-service basis.

Learn Your Learning Style — VIS.2

As you develop your own effective study habits, you will benefit from understanding a little about your personal learning style and your mode of information-processing. Each of us has a unique approach to learning, some of which is determined by the nature of our personalities. For example, consider the visual/ auditory/ kinesthetic distinction (VAK)...

Visual learners primarily use their visual sense to absorb and process information. High visuals like to watch, read, and see notes, overheads, posters, and videos. You can recognize a high visual through his or her language; they might say, "Oh, I see what you mean." "I can't see the point of this." "Look at me." Visual learners often talk quickly. They absorb a great deal of information by reading textbooks and other written materials.

Auditory learners are more likely to use hearing as their modus operandi. Listening, talking, discussing ideas (and even talking to themselves) helps them understand and remember. They say, "OK, OK, I hear you." "I hear you got chosen for the team." "Listen to me." Auditory learners talk more slowly. They absorb a great deal of information by listening to lectures and other verbal teaching styles.

Kinesthetic learners move around, touch, fidget, and play with objects as they absorb information. They are often hands-on, "do it," learners, taking a physically active part in their learning. They say, "I get you." "Give this a try." "I feel stuck." "Do as I do." Kinesthetic learners may talk even more slowly and deliberately, or they may use gestures instead of words. A high kinesthetic learns best by doing.

Most of you will use a combination of all three modalities, but you'll be dominant in one. So will your professors. In class, your instructor may rely heavily on his or her preferred modality, and it may not match yours. Be strategic! Make each class work for you and your information processing style! You may need to add your own twists...

- If you are a high visual, sit near the front of the class where you can see. Remember your information by reading your textbooks and notes, looking at the pictures and diagrams, and using coloured markers to make your notes visually interesting.
- If you are a high auditory, sit where you can hear well (perhaps the front or middle of the room, in the centre), listen, ask questions, discuss, and, if you have permission, tape-record the class. Remember your information by reciting, talking, questioning and listening to tapes.
- As a kinesthetic learner, you will learn best by moving around. Choose a place near the back of the room, so that you don't distract others. Use a squeeze

Hints

Study Tips for Science, Math, and other Technical Subjects — You may be a bit rusty, so consider using your high school texts as a refresher on the basics. You'll need study to understand, and regular practice to remember. Use flash cards to learn the formulae. Be sure you understand how each formula is derived and what it means. Create your own charts and diagrams to capture key information. As with any subject, keep up by reviewing regularly!

ball or play dough, write, doodle, draw, flex your fingers, join in activities and hands-on projects. To remember: walk around, touch and handle objects, type, word process, or model-build as you learn. Get into a rhythm: squeezing a small ball in your hand rhythmically or walking.

Rationalists, Idealists, Guardians, and Artisans

As you might imagine, there is more to learning style than VAK. Personality type is also relevant to this discussion. As you'll know if you've ever taken a psychology course, personality typing is a actually a book (or several hundred books) unto itself. Following is simply a quick introduction to the topic; our intention here is to help you know yourself and your learning style just a little better. After looking at and thinking about the checklists below, you may have some insight into why you make the choices you do, how you interpret the world around you, what you notice and respond to, and where you get your energy.

A word of caution: none of these styles predicts success or determines intelligence. None is "better" than the other. They do, however, influence how you learn, as well as accounting for that different perspective you may have on a situation.

Researchers have identified four major personality types, which are sometimes labeled with the somewhat obscure terms Rationalist, Idealist, Guardian, and Artisan. Take a moment to decide which type fits you by checking the items, in all four styles, that best describe you.

C

RATIONALISTS are: ✔	IDEALISTS are: ✔
❏ visionaries, futurists ❏ 'big picture' people ❏ theoretical,philosophical ❏ analytical thinkers ❏ perfectionists ❏ systematic ❏ inquisitive ❏ independent ❏ persistent ❏ competent and complex ❏ serious ❏ knowledge seekers	❏ persuasive ❏ enthusiastic ❏ team and group people ❏ people-oriented ❏ optimistic ❏ sensitive to others ❏ seekers of harmony ❏ encouraging ❏ expressive ❏ imaginative ❏ motivating ❏ growth oriented

GUARDIANS are: ✔	ARTISANS are: ✔
❏ organized and orderly ❏ predictable ❏ consistent ❏ specialized ❏ dependable and reliable ❏ perfectionist ❏ loyal and service-oriented ❏ more comfortable with the status quo ❏ detail-oriented ❏ structured ❏ conservative and stable ❏ security conscious ❏ respectful of authority	❏ self-confident ❏ decision makers ❏ challengers ❏ results-focused ❏ problem solvers ❏ competitive ❏ independent ❏ practical ❏ creative ❏ humorous ❏ in need of visibility ❏ negotiators ❏ action-oriented

Recognizing your type will help you to make use of specific strategies to enhance your learning and memory. Research indicates that each of us has a dominant brain hemisphere that influences how we learn. Rationalists and Guardians tend to be **Left Brain Dominant** or **Logic Dominant.** Idealists and Artisans tend to be **Right Brain Dominant** or **Gestalt (whole picture) Dominant.** (As with all research, remember there are exceptions!)

Typically, Logic-Dominant people (rationalists and guardians) are more logical, rational, analytical, detail-oriented, and specific. By contrast, Gestalt-Dominant people (idealists and artisans) are more intuitive, emotional, creative, and holistic. The trick to effective and efficient learning is to practice using some of the attributes of the opposite side of the brain. This will help you integrate the activities and functions of both sides, and increase your learning potential!

For example, if you are an *Idealist* or an *Artisan,* use some of these activities to help you become more *orderly* and *analytical* in your thinking by tapping into the opposite side of your brain:

- Manage your time.
- Make schedules and lists.
- Prioritize.
- Use flow charts to sequence.
- Deal with the details.
- Finish the projects or tasks that you start.
- Analyze situations.
- Reason logically.
- Use objective measurements—10:23 a.m., 4.5 km.
- List advantages and disadvantages and give them weighted values.
- Make outlines, draw diagrams and pictures, use mind maps to clarify and break the whole into parts.
- Use sequences when you think and speak: "we will deal with 3 issues: 1st........; 2nd........; finally......"
- Memorize by using tunes, rhythms, mnemonics, and jumping or skipping.

On the other hand, if you are a *Guardian* or *Rationalist,* these strategies will help you tap into the *creative, intuitive* capacities which you are less inclined to use automatically:

- Brainstorm ideas.
- Listen to your 'gut feelings,' instincts and intuition.
- Visualize patterns, pictures, situations with your 'mind's eye.'
- Use symbol and picture mind maps, rather than words.

- Talk about your feelings and emotions.
- Write songs, poems, verse with colorful images and no rhyme or rhythm.
- Swim, walk, rollerblade, hike and participate in non-competitive activities.
- Use stories, symbols and metaphors when you talk ("I was as excited as a kid in a candy store").
- Practice coping with paradoxes and ambiguities (situations that have several potential outcomes, rather than 'black and white' solutions).
- Talk more slowly, if you are a fast talker.
- Dance, sculpt, do pottery, play with colour and clay in free-form movement.
- Try role-playing situations, to understand the 'big picture' or the context.

You may recognize crucial elements in your roommate's style, or observe your professors and figure out what styles they favour. This can aid communication and understanding by giving you clues about what's important to them.

Preparing for Exams — VIS.3

- **We can help you to become a successful exam writer.**
- **(Want to know more?)**
- **There are five, simple, basic, essential steps.**
- **Read on...**

Step 1: Prepare Early for Exams (read: start the first day of school)

We are probably not the first people to suggest this to you. That's because it's really good advice! Lots of students wait until the last minute to study (read: cram) for tests and exams. By then, their notes are unrecognizable and the course material is mostly forgotten. This means they must relearn old material, instead of simply reviewing it. Of course at that point there is no time left to get help, or to make up for material you don't have.

Course outlines and reading lists can seem overwhelming. The temptation to delay, to postpone the pain, is often strong. But as thousands of students would tell you, the pain gets a lot worse that way. You will have accumulated a vast amount of material to cover. Make it easier on yourself, and your grades. Plan short and medium-range goals to organize your work for the term.

Develop a master calendar. Assign yourself manageable 'chunks' of work each week, and be sure to include cumulative reviews throughout the semester. Enter all your deadlines for assignments and tests, as well as your review plan, in your master calendar. Your reviews should cover all the materials, both from class and your texts. Some students use coloured markers to differentiate between subjects, or to highlight tests. Experiment and see what works for you.

Start reviewing on your first day of classes, and make it a habit to do so every day! Spend a half-hour or so in the evening reviewing the entire day's notes. This may also help you get 'psyched up' to do your homework or tackle an assignment.

Step 2: Study smart, not hard (this isn't quite a war, but strategy is everything)

We all know the basic study strategies: *reading and re-reading* textbooks and notes, *memorizing* passages out of textbooks and notes, *copying* and *recopying* notes. These are appropriate for some study situations, but definitely not for all. If you are required to reproduce sections of your textbook verbatim, or memorize specific details for multiple-choice exams, or recite and reproduce specific formulae, then use these techniques–*and only then.*

Be smart. It is more effective to find out from your professor or TA what specific skills, behaviours and knowledge will be tested on the exam. Then, if you are required to solve math problems, for example, learn and understand the formulae, and practice using them to solve specific problems. If you are required to "compare and contrast" two sets of information, poems, theories, or whatever, then practice this strategy. If you will be required to recognize details in multiple choice questions, get out the flash cards (and see the section on multiple choice exams below).

Check old exam questions. Instructors will often provide you with samples of past exams, if you ask. Some depart-ments (or students' unions) also keep back files of old

C

exams. Or you can talk to students who have taken the course and ask them about the instructor's preferences and exam style. Don't get caught, though — be sure to prepare for your exam rather than confining yourself to the content required by old exams. Contrary to many myths, professors do prepare new exam questions!

Consider your professor's style. Some professors emphasize the details, using lots of dates, names, statistics, quantities, and the like. They care about the minutiae — the pieces that make up the whole. Your job will be to learn these details, tedious as that may be. If you catch yourself saying, "He would never ask something as picky as that on an exam," think again. With this type of professor, that may be precisely what will happen. When your professor likes detail, flash cards work well. Pieces of information, details, and dates can all be recorded and memorized. (Of course, it is still important for you to understand what you have learned. After all, there is a bigger purpose here!)

If your professor is more focussed on the big picture — how things fit together, the concepts behind the details, global thinking — then use that approach to learn your material. In this case, learn more rather than less. You seriously increase your risk of a poor grade if you try to get away with a minimalist approach. If your professor is global in outlook, throw away your flash cards. You will need to understand and be able to apply the material, rather than simply recognize it.

Either way, never assume that your instructor won't ask something simply because she or he hasn't covered it in class. Assume always that you are responsible for knowing the material in your textbooks and readings, whether or not that material was specifically mentioned. The first exam is usually the one that sets the style for exams to follow. If you do poorly on the first test, adjust your studying accordingly.

Listen carefully for the hints! Often, teachers describe their testing styles, or give hints on what they expect to find in your answers. Of course, teachers love to do this when a third of the class is away skiing...

Step 3: Get feedback on assignments, tests, presentations, and your thinking

Ask your professor or TA for comments on how to improve your work. Understand and record your errors. Learn from your mistakes! Participate in class discussions and learn from different points of view. Review "model answers."

Become part of a study group. Meet regularly. Work together to prepare for exams. Collect and review information for assignments. Studying with a group has decided advantages. You can clarify material you don't understand; test ideas; get comments and feedback on assignments; ask and answer potential exam questions. Support and encourage each other.

Study groups need to stay focused and task-oriented. They work only if everyone 'pulls their weight' and co-operates. This is not a good place for slackers. If conflicts occur, be prepared to resolve them amicably, or dissolve the group. You don't want to be playing mental games that distract you from learning.

Caution: This does not mean doing work for someone else, or getting them to do your work and then passing it off as your own. That is plagiarism — which is unethical, unacceptable, not smart, and punishable by the university.

Step 4: Take Care of Yourself — Physically, Mentally and Emotionally

More students get sick before and during exams than at any other time. (Or they work like crazy for weeks and get sick the minute the last exam ends.) This is more than predictable, it is also preventable!

Get regular sleep. (Read: eight or nine hours every night!) You will retain more information, manage stress more effectively, and feel more alive. No one wins through sleep deprivation — in fact, you can lose big. Researchers at the University of British Columbia found that students' IQs actually drop when they are deprived of sleep. Normally, teens require nine or ten hours of sleep, but average around seven. For each hour of sleep under eight hours, you lose one point in IQ. For each hour below seven, you can lose two points of IQ. And that's cumulative. (If you are an average student and cheat on your sleep by two hours a night for a week, when your Friday exam rolls around you will have lost 15 IQ points. You are now going into the exam as a below average student.)

This is reversible: if you do lose sleep, try to make it up soon. ***Do your brain a favour — get plenty of sleep!***

Eat proper meals. Food is the fuel for your working body and mind. Eat regularly, choose healthy foods, and drink plenty of water. Drink a large glass of water before you start to study, and at regular intervals throughout the day (at least eight glasses a day is recommended). Are we starting to sound like your parents yet?

Get appropriate exercise. Walk, ride your bike, stretch, go to aerobics or work out regularly. It keeps you fit, alert, strengthens your immune system, and reduces depression.

Nourish healthy relationships. Build healthy relation-ships with friends, romantic attachments, parents and relatives. Reduce contacts with those people who cause you unnecessary pain or stress, and distract you from your studies. Take care of your feelings! Use your Student Counselling Services if you need help or support.

Step 5: Seek Balance!

Have realistic expectations about what you can accomplish. Be vigilant against self-defeating attitudes and beliefs (those nasties "I can't," "I must," and "I'll never" especially). Replace them with "I can," "I choose to," and "I will."

Take time each week to socialize and have fun. Schedule down time! The break from your books and computer will revitalize you.

Jake is a big picture person. He likes themes, ideas, large concepts. He tends to skip over the details (because they seem obvious). His first multiple-choice exam results were a disaster. He complained that the questions were picky, too detailed, and asked for irrelevant details. At a subsequent study-skills workshop, he became aware that learning the details, and remembering the picky facts, was part of the skill he needed to answer the professor's multiple-choice questions successfully. He grumbled, but he used the new strategy anyway. His marks in the class improved dramatically, in spite of the fact that his overall style is still that of the big picture person.

Laugh a lot (closely related to socializing and having fun). Keep your sense of humour and optimism. Laughter is healing, both for your body and for your mind! The blackest day looks sunnier, if you can laugh about it.

Get help when you need it. If you are overwhelmed, or can't cope with your personal, social or academic life, see a counsellor at Student Counselling Services. They are there to help you. You don't need to wait for a crisis; go sooner rather than later.

Specific Strategies for Specific Exams — VIS.4

First, the often-dreaded Multiple Choice:

Multiple choice exams are a fact of student life. Some students love them; others hate them. Either way, here are our tips for mastering the art of the multiple choice question...

1. Divide the number of multiple choice questions into the amount of time you have available, so that you know how much time you can spend on each question.

2. If you have a mixed exam (part multiple choice and part essay) start by reading all the questions. Estimate which part of the exam is worth the most marks, and make sure you allocate your time proportionately. The questions worth the most marks should get the biggest percentage of your time.

3. Now work through each question. Begin by reading the question carefully and thoroughly.

4. Underline the key words in the question.

5. Formulate an answer in your head.

6. Look carefully at all the choices, particularly if you get options like "all of the above," "none of the above," "a & c" or "b & d."

7. Cross off the choices you have never seen before in the course text or notes, and cross off the choices that are obviously wrong.

8. Narrow your choices down to two.

9. Remember that the "best answer" is not the same as the "right answer." The term "right answer" assumes that all other answers are wrong. The term "best answer" suggests there may be more than one right answer. Whenever you are asked to choose "the best answer," you will need to apply your knowledge to distinguish between "right answers."

10. At times, there may also be the "professor's answer." If you miss that one, but you can argue your choice and back it up with course information, you may be able to raise your grade by explaining why you chose the answer you did.

11. If you are unsure of the answer, make a note in the margin and come back to that question later. (Your mind continues to process information while you are working on the next questions.) Make sure you come back to the question and at least guess (as long as you aren't penalized for guessing). Don't leave blanks unless you are specifically warned that marks are subtracted for wrong answers. Guessing can give you up to a 50% chance to get the answer right.

Now, the Essay Questions:

First, the preliminaries: be ready, know your materials well, be prepared to "contrast and compare," or "review and discuss." Be sure you understand what instructions such as these actually mean: "analyze," "develop," "outline," "explain," "define," and "demonstrate." Check the definitions in your dictionary and practice using these words in your projects and papers. Review old exam questions, or develop some questions yourself, and practice writing essays using your study materials.

Once you get to the exam...

1. Read the general instructions before you look at the essay questions. Then read all the essay questions carefully. Be sure you understand them. Jot down any trigger words that come to mind as you read each question, and keep making cryptic notes as you continue.

2. Choose the question you feel you can answer best and start with that. If you can't decide, write down the points you remember for each, and then make a choice.

3. If you lose an idea, let it go. It will come back. Write down any word associations or acronyms in the margin to help trigger your memory.

4. Approach each question logically and systematically. Jot down an outline, or use a mind map to order your information properly. Start with your main argument and build the essay from there, using points to support your perspective. Allow for new ideas that might pop up while you are writing, and add them.

5. Always answer the question that was asked. Write everything you know about the question that is relevant. Don't assume that details are not important or that your professor already knows that information. The professor wants to know what you know. It's a waste of valuable time to add unrelated information that might suggest you're padding your answer.

6. Save a few minutes at the end to review your essay answers, and add any data that come to mind. Check your grammar and spelling, and correct those errors you notice.

7. Answer all the questions you are required to. If you are running out of time, quickly write down an out line and some specific points. At least you've indicated that you have knowledge about this question, which will get you some marks. Use all the time allotted to you. Be the last, rather than the first, out of the exam room.

A Very Important Note:
Most schools recognize that not everyone learns or processes information at the same pace, or in the same way. If you have a learning disability, or you need more time to answer tests, talk to your professor. Frequently, arrangements can be made to give you more time or to test you in another room. If you need to use special tools (notebook computer, tape recorder, or whatever), again be sure to talk with your professor ahead of time, so that appropriate arrangements can be made.

Our Best Exam-Taking Pointers:

1. *Sleep well the night before.* Cramming and all-nighters will often let you down the next day. We all forget more easily when we are tired or over-stimulated.

2. *Be prepared.* Do your studying and reviewing, systematically and methodically, throughout the semester. Feel ready!

3. *Be confident* that you know the information and can access it easily when you need it. Use positive affirmations to remind you of your competence: try "I am confident and competent." "I have all the information I need." "I can access this information when I need it."

4. *Avoid clusters of panicking students* who compare what they don't know and scramble to collect last minute tidbits of information from each other. One scrap of extra data will not make much difference, if you haven't done your homework! Fear and panic is contagious. Find a quiet spot and focus inward. Stay calm, centered, and balanced. Or find someone else who seems calm and prepared, and chat about non-test-related topics.

5. *When you enter the exam room, stay calm.* Choose your seat, and keep your focus. Check for any general instructions that might be posted on your table or on the chalkboard, and make sure you

understand them. Listen to all verbal instructions; ask for clarification if needed.

6. ***When you get your question sheet, read all the instructions and questions thoroughly.*** Give yourself time to read through the whole paper, and make any quick notes or reminders you need. If a question is unclear, ask the professor for clarification.

7. ***Look carefully to see if there are any choices or optional questions.*** You will not get extra marks for writing answers to more questions than necessary. If the exam stipulates four out of five questions are to be answered, that is exactly what it means. Only your first four answers will be graded.

8. ***Calculate the amount of time you have available to complete each question.*** Spend more time on those questions that are worth the most marks. Start with the questions you know best and can answer well. If you can't answer a question, come back to it later.

9. ***Your mind will process several questions at once.*** If points come to mind, go back and jot them down next to the appropriate question. Write all you know that is relevant. Details are important. They indicate you have studied the material.

10. ***If all else fails, guess!*** (unless you get penalized for wrong answers).

11. ***Watch the time.*** Stay until the end. Be the last person to leave, rather than making a dramatic exit after the first half hour. This will not be a waste of time. You may draw a blank at first, but as you calm down, centre yourself, and focus your attention, your memory will kick into action, and you will be able to write. If you finish before the time runs out, use those minutes to review and make sure you have not missed anything.

12. ***Let go of fear, and find your centre within. You can only succeed.***

Avoiding the First Trap:
The Fine Art Of Scheduling

The majority of students who fail at university do so not because they are incapable of handling the intellectual demands of a university program, but because they lack effective time management. Your greatest asset lies in learning how to organize and manage your time wisely. If you do so, you will have control over your life. You will be able to get your work done and still have time for socializing. You will be working smart, rather than merely working hard.

We all have the same amount of time: 168 hours a week. How you use those hours is what makes the difference. A smart, strategic, creative schedule will help you avoid many of the common mistakes that plague university students.

The first step in scheduling your time is to draft a monthly schedule. (The month-at-a-glance reusable charts available in most university bookstores are great for this.) Write down all your important dates, including the time of classes; due dates for assignments, essays, and exams; and any appointments you have made for the month. Update this chart weekly, and include weekends.

The 'Unschedule'...

Now use the Unschedule. Every week you will need a separate unschedule on a master sheet. (The hourly segmented, week-at-a-glance reusable sheets work well here.) Your master sheet should break each day into half-hour segments. Fill in class, lab, and tutorial hours. Then enter all other regular activity hours, including your job, sports, workouts, club meetings, and the like. Finally, add household activities such as meals, chores, and even sleep. You have now scheduled all your committed time.

Your weekly unschedule now also reflects your uncommitted time. How will you use it? First, create blocks of study time. (You might use coloured markers to represent the hours for each course.) Then schedule social activities and other time off. Evaluate your schedule each weekend. If you feel unsatisfied with your results in an area, modify your time allocation. Choices and trade-offs are inevitable. Sometimes you will need more study and less socializing, other times it will be the reverse. The boundaries you must work within are non-negotiable; no one can bargain for more than 168 hours a week!

WEEKLY UN-SCHEDULE   Week Of: _____

	MON	TUE	WED	THU	FRI	SAT	SUN
7 AM			S A M P L E		Dentist		
8		Bio Lab		P/T Job	↓	P/T Job	
9	Bio 101 ↓	↓	Bio 101 ↓		Bio 101 ↓		
10	Econ 320 ↓	↓	Econ 320 ↓		Econ 320 ↓		Bike w/Sandy
11	Study Psyc		Study Humn	↓	Read Bio Chap 2		↓
Noon	Lunch ↓	Lunch Humn 305	Lunch ↓	Lunch Humn 305	Lunch ↓		
1 PM		↓		↓			Study for Midterms
2	Workout	Psyc 255	Workout	Psyc 255	Workout		↓
3	↓ Meet	↓	↓	Research	Groceries		Laundry & Review
4	Bio TA	P/T Job	Grp Proj. Meeting	Paper		↓	Notes
5	Type Bibliog		↓	↓		Study for Midterms	↓
6	Dinner		Dinner	Dinner	Dinner	↓	Dinner
7	Dance Class			Study			
8	↓	↓					
9			Movie w/ Bob	↓		Party at Stacey's	
10			↓				

More Specific Scheduling Suggestions...

onsultants

You may be an experienced scheduler (lots of parents have learned to be!). If so, you might show your client how your scheduling system works for you (acknowledging, of course, that this is just one of several options). If your client is interested, you could try some scheduling together, keeping in mind his needs, style and preferences. Ask questions like:

- *What tasks and activities do you want to schedule?*
- *How much can you commit to at this point?*
- *What are your stress points?*
- *What do you need to help you stay on schedule?*

Respect your client - allow him to set the dates, choose the tasks, make the adjustments and evaluate the process.

1. Write a daily Task List (which fits into your weekly Unschedule), either the night before or first thing in the morning. Note everything you have to do that day. Divide these tasks according to three levels of priority: A (high priority), B (middle priority), and C (low priority). An "A" priority is an essay that is due in two days. A "C" priority might include filing notes or reorganizing work space. The "A" tasks should be done first, followed by "B" and then "C." If you avoid your "A" work and justify your actions by completing "C" chores, you are procrastinating.

2 Allow yourself a comfortable amount of time to do your normal morning activities such as showering, dressing, eating, and getting to class. Avoid getting up at the last minute and rushing to class with your 'bad hair' under a baseball cap! The whole day tends to unfold chaotically after that.

3. Try to start working as soon as you reach school. Treat school like a job.

4. Find a quiet place on campus to study in your free periods, and use it regularly. If you use your school hours for school work, you will have more free hours to use for your own enjoyment, rather than for hectic studying.

5. The number of hours you need for school work depends on the type of person you are and the course load you carry. As a starting point, try to allot three study hours for every hour that you spend in class. Schedule these hours for maximum productivity. For example, study just before class if you will be expected to discuss the material — that way it's fresh in your mind. If your class involves extensive note-taking and new material, review the notes as soon as possible after the class — you will reinforce recent learning. (This is most important if the material is difficult. Naturally, it takes longer to process more difficult information.)

C

6. Live by the most regular schedule you can. Since you are treating school as you would a job, give yourself time for lunch and at least an hour after the day's work to relax and eat supper, before you begin to study again. Perhaps you might exercise after work, catch up on social calls, or just read the newspaper. Don't exhaust yourself! After dinner, start in on your homework.

7. Spend two or three hours studying each night, using 50-minute study blocks followed by 10-minute breaks. Avoid studying when you are exhausted. Set a time limit and stick to it, so that you will have a good night's sleep. If you are a morning person, try getting up early — maybe 5:00 a.m. actually suits you — and studying before breakfast. That could free up your evenings, when you are tired after a long day and not at your concentrating best. Weekends, for most students, are not free time. You will need to use at least some of that time for studying, and maybe a part-time job. ·

**Student reality is usually a busy,
7-day work and study week
with less free time than you might expect.
This is your investment in your future!**

R eal Life

Julie felt overloaded and overwhelmed. She simply did not have time for everything: five courses, a part-time job, volunteer commitments, a social life, exercise, and homework. To make matters worse, her parents didn't understand her problem — when they were at university in the 1960s, they had fun, free time, and still graduated. Julie agreed to try the 'Unschedule.' To her surprise, she found that she had more activities to schedule than she had hours available in the week. The only way to fit everything in was to 'borrow' from her sleep time — not a good idea. Instead, she re-evaluated. She reduced her volunteer hours, withdrew from one course, and re-arranged her social plans. She created the balance she needed.

Are You A Morning Person?
Check the following statements, if they apply to you...
I like to be up early in the morning.
  ❏ *Always*   ❏ *Sometimes*   ❏ *Never*

I have lots of energy in the morning.
  ❏ *Always*   ❏ *Sometimes*   ❏ *Never*

I learn easily and concentrate well in the morning.
  ❏ *Always*   ❏ *Sometimes*   ❏ *Never*

I like to run/jog/walk/exercise in the morning.
  ❏ *Always*   ❏ *Sometimes*   ❏ *Never*

I enjoy breakfast.
  ❏ *Always*   ❏ *Sometimes*   ❏ *Never*

I concentrate poorly in the evening.
  ❏ *Always*   ❏ *Sometimes*   ❏ *Never*

I have difficulty staying awake late in the evening.
  ❏ *Always*   ❏ *Sometimes*   ❏ *Never*

I have to re-do work when I study at night.
  ❏ *Always*   ❏ *Sometimes*   ❏ *Never*

If you answered always to four or more questions, you are probably a 'morning person,' or at least you can train yourself to become efficient in the morning.

Know Your Scheduling Pitfalls...

1. **Procrastination** — delaying until later something that should be done today is a common mistake. Follow your monthly, weekly, and daily schedules. Try not to change your plans just because you are anxious or find the task a burden. Avoid the excuse that you "work best under pressure" — for most people, that is just a juicy rationalization. Too little time to do a good job usually results in a mediocre grade.

2. **Poor Concentration** — If you concentrate, then any task need be done only once. Motivate yourself! Treat schoolwork as a job to be done by a certain deadline. Reward yourself with a treat if you finish

early or on time: a TV show, a walk or bike ride, a chat with a friend (maybe even a chocolate bar). Be attentive, remove all distractions, and stick to the study habits we've described. Discourage interruptions by ignoring the phone or using an answering machine while you're studying.

3. **Fatigue and Boredom** — Try working in study segments of 50 minutes, followed by a 10-minute break. If you are not being effective, allow yourself to take a break, switch to something else, or go to bed. Early-morning study may be a good alternative for you.

4. **Trying to do it all** — Plan your tasks, and know which ones are important. Don't be afraid to say "no" to unimportant tasks or requests. Avoid getting overburdened, or pleasing others, to your disadvantage.

5. **Time Wasters** — We all have to wait for buses, appointments, or classes. Carry a book, notes, audio tapes or flash cards with you so that you can utilize this transition time productively. Alternatively, you can use waiting time to practice being centered and relaxed.

Please Remember...

Your schedule is a guideline. It is not cast in stone. If, after the first week, you're having trouble getting your work done — or if you are done more quickly than you expected — then revise your schedule. Don't become a slave to something that isn't working. When you adjust your schedule, notice where you tended to waste time, deviate, or accomplish less than you expected — and make some changes. If you accomplished less than you wanted, for example, try dividing the time slots into smaller chunks and diversify what you study when. Perhaps your goals are unrealistic. Revise, restructure, and then stick to the new schedule. You'll find yourself becoming an effective manager of time.

Avoiding the Second Trap:
Keep Your Eye on the Ball
(setting goals and staying motivated)

Our purpose in this section is to give you some tools which will help keep you going, when the going gets tough. There is no doubt that post-secondary education is a great deal of work. For many people, this will be one of the most intense work periods of their lives. So how do you keep moving, stay on track, and have faith that you'll get there? One of the best ways, of course, is to always be clear about where you're going. This means taking some time to set your personal goals.

There are big goals, which will take years to achieve, and there are smaller goals, which can be achieved in the not-too-distant future. Your "big goal" is probably the main reason you are in school, for example...
  "To earn my bachelor's degree in..."
  "To complete my education and training as a ..."
  "To earn the credentials to work in..."

These are great goals. They are also a few years away. Looking ahead four years can feel remote and unreal. So much can — and usually does — happen, between now and then. The further away your goal, the less control you have over all the possible intervening circumstances.

On the other hand, the closer your goal is to today, the more control you have over your ability to achieve it. For this reason, it is crucial to break your big goal down into smaller pieces, with shorter time frames, and work towards each one. Picture each of the pieces as a stepping stone on the path to your ultimate destination.

Task⇨task⇨task⇨task⇨task⇨task⇨BigGoal

You determine what each of these tasks — your smaller, short term goals — need to be, by working backwards from your big goal. In other words, what are all the steps you need to take in order to make that big goal happen?

YOU ARE HERE ⇦ ⇦ ⇦ **YOUR GOAL**

Once you have identified all the tasks or action steps you need to take, you can implement them in a forward direction. The tasks or action steps needed to reach your big goal become your short-term and intermediate goals.

YOU ARE HERE   task1   task2   task3   YOUR GOAL

For example, if your big goal is to graduate with a B.A. in four years, there are several specific things you need to do this semester, in order to keep moving in the direction of your future. Define your goals for the current semester. Then subdivide those goals into monthly goals, weekly goals and daily tasks. For each task, you need to establish a time frame — goals don't mean much unless they are placed within a period of time. This is where your time management skills come into play. (Review our section on managing time, if you need help there.)

Your goals for each course this term might look something like this...

You Are Here ⇨ ⇨ ⇨ ⇨ ⇨ ⇨ ⇨ ⇨ ⇨ ⇨ ⇨ **Your Goal: An 'A' In English**

Attend class	Complete assignment	Write midterm	Get a tutor	Study for final	Write exam

Then you add the appropriate time frames or deadlines...

Semester Goals	Tasks	Completion
"A" IN ENGLISH	Complete Assignment 1	Oct 15
	Study for Mid-term	Oct 30
	Complete Assignment 2	Nov 30
	Study for Final	Dec 19
"A" IN PSYCH	Complete Questionnaire	Oct 4
	Study for Quiz 1	Oct 9
	Study for Quiz 2	Oct 23
	Study for Mid-term	Oct 31
	Study for Quiz 3	Nov 23
	Study for Final	Dec 15

And so on, for each of your other courses. Finally, you enter each task in your Unschedule, setting aside enough time each week that you can accomplish the goal you have set for yourself within the time available.

This plan will only work if you work it. It takes commitment to "plan the work and work the plan." No one else will police you, or check to see whether you are meeting your own expectations. Your expectations of yourself are your own! Professors set the deadlines — it is, of course, up to you to get the work done on time. Your reward is the achievement of your goal!

Stay Inspired! Maintain Hope! Reach for the Stars! The Magic of Motivation

The trickiest thing about motivation is that you need it most when you feel it least. Here, then, are some tricks of the trade on maintaining that essential quality, personal motivation.

Humans are naturally motivated in one of two ways:
1. We are motivated to act to avoid pain or discomfort (for example, failing an exam, missing a bus, feeling hungry).
2. We are motivated to act to achieve pleasure (for example, earning a good grade, winning a race, arranging a party).

In both cases, we act, and we are responsible for the outcome. Avoiding pain or achieving pleasure is in our hands.

"So how do I motivate myself?"
You may have noticed that you talk to yourself sometimes. You may not have noticed how much. In fact, people are often unaware of the 'little voice in the head' that maintains a steady chatter throughout the day. Most of us hardly notice what we are telling ourselves with that little voice. You can be sure, however, that your state of mind and being is profoundly affected by this self talk — for better or for worse.

If the self talk from that little voice in the head is negative, you are almost certain to feel negative - discouraged, hopeless, stupid, ugly, afraid. Your mind will believe what you tell it. If you bombard yourself with negative thoughts, your mind accepts those thoughts as truth. Most people have practiced negative self talk on themselves for years, so it is easy to see why they become negative and unmotivated.

The good news is that negative self talk is completely reversible. *You can choose what you tell yourself. You can practice positive self talk. You can become intentional in your thinking.* You can therefore affect how you feel, react, and respond. The key is to consciously change your self talk habits. The essential tools in this transformation are:
1. becoming aware of what you tell yourself;
2. choosing another, more positive message;
3. repeating the new message firmly and convincingly to yourself; and
4. writing it down where you can see it often.

New habits need practice, if they are to become a part of you. Sometimes, you need to "fake it until you make it." In other words, even if you don't believe your new positive self talk immediately, keep on using it. You can and will develop a new belief system.

Shifting Negative Self Talk... some specifics:

My professor is boring.	becomes...	**My professor is knowledgeable and I'm learning a lot.**
I don't like this course.	becomes...	**I like this course more as I learn more.**
I am stupid.	becomes...	**I am competent and intelligent.**
I can't understand this.	becomes...	**I choose to get help in learning this material.**

This may feel forced at first, but the rewards are worth it. There are enough obstacles in the outside world. You don't need to create extra obstacles for yourself inside your head!

"What if I don't feel the motivation to get up in the morning?"

You are probably in good company, but that doesn't solve your problem. Start with the practical. Check your late night habits. Are you getting enough sleep (read: eight or nine hours)? Then check your purpose. Ask yourself, *"Why am I here? What is my goal?"* "Why am I at university, instead of earning five dollars an hour flipping hamburgers?" Finally, check your self talk. If you tell yourself you are not a morning person, there is no way you will ever become one!

Try behaving "as if." Sometimes, it is helpful to behave "as if" you want to do something, or "as if" you are interested, happy, excited, and energetic, or "as if" you really can get up with the sun in the morning. Your mind actually doesn't know the difference between what you believe, and what you tell yourself you believe. Practice behaving "as if," and you will begin to genuinely feel that way. Trust us on this one!

This is also a good place for "one day at a time." *Just for today,* I will get up and go to class. *Just for today*, I will pay attention and make it worth my while. *Just for today,* I will plan my work and work my plan.

The Power of Thinking Positive — Using Affirmations

Affirmations are positive, active statements which you tell yourself, and which you repeat as often as you can. Affirmation statements become almost like a chant, as you say them over and over. This is positive self talk in action, changing your old, familiar negative self talk into something alive and motivating.

Choose a few positive statements that are appropriate for your current state of mind and the activity at hand. As you sit down to study, for example, you might repeat over and over to yourself for a moment or two: "I am alert and aware." Before you go into an exam, you might try, "I can access all the knowledge I need," or "I am calm and confident." Always phrase affirmation statements in the present tense, to remind yourself that this is the here and now, and that you are actively engaged.

Affirmations work, if you use them regularly and consistently. Here are our suggestions — useful affirmations with positive impact for the many students who have used them to stay motivated:

I am an excellent student.
I can learn anything and everything.
I am winning.
I am competent and confident.
I am relaxed and alert.
I am alert and aware.
I am energetic and efficient.
I am working efficiently for my A Grade.
I enjoy learning new things.
I am terrific (or great, or super).

Choose your own affirmations. Experiment until you find statements that are comfortable, and easy to remember when you need them. Say them to yourself, write them down repetitively, and be creative — make posters, draw pictures, post them in places where you will see them often. Affirmations belong above your desk, on your mirror, on the refrigerator, at the top of each page in your note book, on the inside of your locker door. The more you remind yourself, the more your mind accepts this as true information, and acts accordingly. It's really quite simple and symmetrical: if you believe you are competent, then you behave competently, and you become competent.

Avoiding the third trap: stress-busting

Nothing saps student effectiveness quite like stress. If you feel 'stressed out,' you simply do not function as well. Your capacity to learn, understand, and remember declines. Your susceptibility to illness increases. And yet stress management is often about taking care of the basics. Here are our favourite stress-busters...

1. Drink lots of water (at least 8 glasses a day). Take a water bottle with you to class every day.
2. Cut down on caffeine, or eliminate it if possible (this includes coffee, tea, colas, and chocolate).

3. Eat healthy foods and minimize the junk food. Try not to skip meals, and don't replace a meal with a sugar snack.
4. Get 8 or 9 hours sleep a night, and keep your intelligence working for you. Too little sleep reduces your intellectual capacity.
5. Exercise — walk across campus, to the store, around the block. Use the campus recreation facilities at your school.
6. Learn to relax. Use a relaxation tape or learn to quiet your mind for at least 15 minutes, twice a day.
7. Problem-solve — when you have a problem, take time to consider all the angles. Ask for help and support, if you need it, to find a creative solution that works for you.
8. Say no to unreasonable requests, or to invitations which don't interest you or you don't have time for.
9. Manage your money carefully, and minimize your impulse buying.
10. Manage your time so that you can keep up with your classes, work, homework and leisure activities.
11. Be kind to yourself. Do nice things for yourself as you would for a friend. Encourage yourself, praise your efforts, reward your achievements, celebrate, listen to your favourite music, visit with good people, take a long hot bath, breathe fresh air on a hill top, watch a sunset.
12. Laugh a lot. Even the worst day looks better, when you can laugh at it.

Our suggestions on study strategies, time management, careful roommate selection — in fact most of the advice in this book — is intended to help minimize the stress of post-secondary education. Our last word on stress... don't sweat the small stuff!

Consultants

A client in stress is difficult to watch. We all want to jump in and save, and we all know this is an impulse to be resisted! The most obvious time to help is when she asks for it. Remember, when she does ask, she may not always need direct assistance. Emotional support is usually welcome and effective. Other times to reach out include...
- *If she is in obvious crisis or danger.*
- *If she's made similar mistakes in the past, and is unable to recognize the pattern.*
- *When she is ill and in need of attention.*
- *If her behaviour has changed noticeably (which could signal depression, drug and alcohol abuse, or other mental illness).*
- *When a financial situation threatens her well-being.*
- *If she is threatened or accused of wrongdoing.*

Times for the consultant to hold back include...
- *When you are specifically asked to keep out.*
- *When your client can do for himself what you are offering to do.*
- *When not helping will encourage him to discover his own ability to problem-solve.*
- *When your need to help becomes the motive, as opposed to his need of your help.*

When you are offering help as a consultant, remember...
- *Listen to your client's concerns, feelings, and fears.*
- *Acknowledge those feelings. "I can see you are upset."*
- *Affirm your client's right to those feelings. "It's understandable to feel like this."*
- *Don't try to fix people, or change what they feel. It's all right for clients to feel what they feel, and then move on.*
- *Know that your emotional support is always appropriate, even when you are choosing to say "no."*

Avoiding the final trap:
Creative Coping with Conflict

You may be surprised to find a section on conflict management in a book about post-secondary education. (It's not as obvious a topic as, say, study skills.) This may make more sense to you the first time you disagree with a fellow student about a joint project you are working on, or after your first really ugly battle with your new roommate, or when you are about to approach an instructor about a grade you want reviewed.

We know two things for sure about conflict. First, each of us has some. Second, each of us has our own attitudes, beliefs, and fears about it. Some examples...
   "A good spat clears the air."
   "I hate arguments. I never win."
   "We argue about such stupid stuff."
   "I stick to my guns. If I know I am right, I say so."
   "We had this fight and then we didn't talk for days. I moved out."
   "She borrowed my notes and gave them back late. I am so angry."
   "I never fight with people."
   "Give a little, take a little. That's what I say."

Conflict occurs when there is a clash between getting your needs and goals met and *keeping your relationships and feelings safe and intact*. Some people like conflict. Most, however, do not. Most of us wish we could live our lives without argument or dissension (possible only in extreme fantasy, or extreme boredom). The problem is usually a lack of skills and tools for creative conflict management. As a result, we experience conflict by feeling helpless, angry, misunderstood, resentful and hurt, when we "lose," *or* triumphant, giddy, superior and elated, when we "win."

Our goal here is to provide effective, user-friendly tools for creative conflict resolution. We begin this process by inviting you to review several typical approaches to conflict, and to recognize yours...

Win-Lose: The traditional approach to conflict is black-and-white competition, as in "I win; you lose," or "I am right; you are wrong." Here there is only room for one winner — everyone else loses and feels bad. If your approach to conflict is fight hard to win, you may achieve your goal and meet your need to win, but you risk damaging your relationship with the person who loses.

Accommodate: Another common approach is to "give in," accommodate, or smooth over the conflict, as in "O.K... you win." (usually in a defeated tone of voice). The attitude here is "I can't win against this person, I want this person to like me, and I don't want anyone to get hurt." If your habit is to accommodate others, you give up on yourself. Eventually, that creates feelings of anger and resentment as you continually "lose" — doing all the giving to the other person's taking.

Avoid: Then there is the avoid-conflict-at-all-costs strategy. Any time you sense an argument about to occur, you withdraw or leave the situation. *"I don't fight,"* or *"Count me out. You two can fight without me. I'm gone."* Unfortunately, though, ignored or avoided problems just keep coming back. Leaving is at best a temporary option. Eventually, you may need to actually resolve that dispute.

Compromise: Many of you have been advised — by your parents or other adults in your life, usually — to "give and take." Give up some of your goals, so that the other person can achieve some of her goals. This can work relatively well, or it can be an arena for resentment. All too often, both parties feel they gave too much, and accomplished too little. Compromise then creates a situation where no one is happy.

Human development strategists suggest a fifth perspective on conflict...the **Win-Win** option. The principle here is that both antagonists achieve their goals (one win) and simultaneously preserve, or even improve, their relationship (another win). Try the following steps to win-win conflict resolution, and see for yourself.

Win-win conflict resolution...(an eight-step circle)
   a) **Calm down, cool off, and call a time out** for both of you. Most conflicts generate a lot of 'heat,' and not much 'light.' Yet, creative problem-solving requires a clear head and a calm heart. Therefore, your first task is to settle down. Leave

the conflict environment, go for a walk, or simply take some deep breaths and count to a hundred (slowly). Agree on a time and place to meet.

b) **Acknowledge the validity and importance of each person's goals,** and state your commitment to work through the problem with respect for feelings and friendship. "Your goals are as important as mine." "I value our relationship." "I will not hurt your feelings intentionally, to get my point across."

c) **Define the problem issue as each of you sees it,** so that you can be sure you are working out the same issue (and not something hidden). "I see the issue as..." "I see it this way..." "It seems that what we really want is..."

d) **Brainstorm all the solutions you can think of,** without editing or censorship. Try not to judge the merits or worth of an idea. Simply write down whatever possibilities occur to you. Let go of any ownership to "your" ideas or solutions.

e) **Evaluate each solution** according to the advantages and disadvantages it presents for each of you. Use a separate sheet of paper for each solution. Divide each sheet into four columns as follows...

Reaching my goal: *Reaching your goal:*
Advantages   *Advantages*
Disadvantages   *Disadvantages*

Eventually you will find a solution that works well for both parties.

f) **Take action on your chosen solution.** Decide how you will implement your plan, who will take responsibility for which actions, what external help you may need, and how you will support each other.

g) **Monitor the solution in action,** to see if it is working well. If your plan needs modification, make the necessary changes and try again. If your plan doesn't work at all, go back to your options and choose another one.

h) **Check back with each other to make sure your solution is working.**

Wayne and Wendy are in conflict. Wendy wants to have friends over on Saturday night, and Wayne needs to study for an exam. Follow the win-win process:

a) *Wayne:* "Wendy, let's have coffee at Tango's and figure out how to deal with Saturday evening."

 Wendy: "O.K. How about after classes at 4?"

b) *Wayne:* "I realize that we share our place, and that you have the right to invite friends over. You pay half the rent."

 Wendy: "Yes — I'm glad you see that. I know that being able to study at home is important to you, too."

c) *Wendy:* "It seems to me that I want to entertain when you want to study, and we can't do both at the same time."

 Wayne: "My top priority is to get through exams. I need to do well so I can get a scholarship."

 Wendy: "I think we're clear on the issue: how do we share the same space and do different things, without making it difficult for each other?"

 Wayne: "Yes! That's it. So, what do we do?"

 Wendy: "Let's think of all our options. Maybe we can find one that works for both of us."

d) *Wayne and Wendy come up with the following options:*
 - *Wendy could entertain her friends a week later.*
 - *The friends could meet at someone else's house.*
 - *Wendy and her friends could go for a bike ride, and then come back to the house for pizza after Wayne is done studying.*
 - *Wayne could go to the library, study until 10:00, and then join in.*
 - *Wayne could study during the day and join the others in the evening.*

e, f, and g) After reviewing the advantages and disadvantages of each solution - for Wayne and for Wendy — they decide together that the bike ride/late pizza solution works best this time. They try it out and find that it works well (Wayne gets his studying done, and everyone has fun). In winter, however, they will need to consider some other options! Solving conflicts using the win-win approach takes time, effort, commitment, and goodwill. The results, however, will be worth it!

**Conflict Resolution Strategies Part 2:
Pillow Talk...**

Here is a strategy you can use either *on your own* (after a disagreement, when you are feeling confused and resentful), or *together* (as a tool for helping you to appreciate the other person's position). Either way, you have the opportunity to see the conflict from the other person's standpoint. It's like walking in his or her shoes.

You need a *table* where you can move around all four sides (coffee, kitchen, or card will do), several sheets of *paper* and a *pencil*.

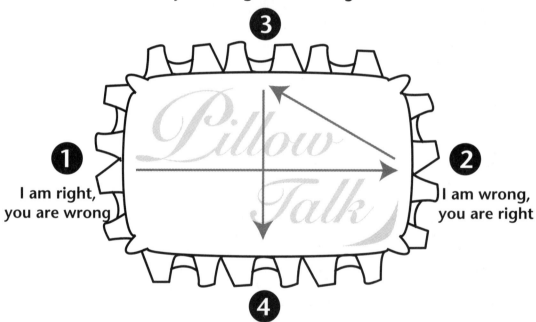

I am right and wrong,
you are right and wrong.

3

I am right,
you are wrong

1

2

I am wrong,
you are right

4

Right and wrong are not important.
They are parts of the same.

First, doing the exercise alone...

1.   Sit at Side 1. On your sheet of paper write down all the reasons why you are *right* and she is *wrong*. (This is easy. You know you are right. That's why you had the fight!)

2.   Now move across the table to Side 2. Look back at where you came from. Write down all the reasons why you are *wrong* and she is *right*. (This is trickier. Do it anyway. You will start to feel an interesting shift in your thinking.)

3.   Move again, this time to Side 3. Write down all the reasons *you are right and wrong, and she is right and wrong.* Usually, this includes some of what you have already written. You may find other reasons, too.

4.   Finally, go to Side 4. Look at where you have been. Notice your feelings — about the disagreement and about the other person. Usually, you will experience a shift, a willingness to recognize that *right and wrong are not important.* At this point, you may be ready to do the exercise with the other person, or try win-win problem-solving.

Now, with the other person... The exercise is the same, except you are talking out loud instead of writing. One person completes the exercise while the other listens, and then you switch. As you move from chair to chair, say out loud why you are right/wrong/right and wrong. The other person listens carefully without responding. Once you have completed your four steps, you change places and reverse roles. When you have both completed the exercise, you will probably feel a lot better. (Have a laugh, a hug, and a better understanding of each other.)

Real Life

Brad and Terri are working on a joint class assignment. They haven't done much planning together, and they have no schedule (a typical case of poor communication). Terri feels that she is doing most of the work, and that Brad is being lazy. They have decided to use Pillow Talk to resolve their conflict. They have cleared the kitchen table, Terri has offered to go first, and Brad is ready to listen.

Terri:
Side 1: I am right, and you are wrong.
1. *I collected all the journal articles.*
2. *I spent two days in the library reading.*
3. *I arranged the meetings with the volunteers.*
4. *I like to have everything organized before we meet.*
5. *It's important to plan ahead and stick to the plan.*
6. *I typed up the rough draft.*
7. *You haven't done your share.*

Side 2: I am wrong, and you are right.
1. *You searched the Internet and found helpful references.*
2. *You changed your work schedule to interview the volunteers next Wednesday.*
4. *You gave me some good suggestions about how to interview.*

Side 3: I am right and wrong. You are right and wrong.
1. *I like to have everything organized and planned, and you are able to 'fly by the seat of your pants.'*
2. *I have done lots of leg work and see you as lazy, but you have a job and less flexible time.*
3. *I have done the planning, but I can't count on you to stick to the plan.*
4. *You always come through, and I need to trust you will this time.*
5. *I typed the rough draft, and you committed to doing all the tables and graphs.*
6. *I get anxious and bug you. You ignore me and don't seem to care.*
7. *I recognize that bugging you doesn't get things done.*
8. *You know that I don't do well under pressure.*

Side 4: The shift... Terri has been around the table, and she feels differently about the situation. Brad really listened to her.

Now Brad takes his turn, and Terri listens. After both have their say, they agree to draw up a schedule which spells out who will do what, when, and how they will support each other to complete the assignment and get a good grade.

C

Our Final Advice: Ask for What You Need

Post-secondary institutions are often large and impersonal. They are not always well prepared to meet the needs of individual students. This does not mean you must be meek and accepting — or, at the other extreme, aggressive and demanding. It is important for you to get what you need from this big bureaucracy. Remember, rules are not always carved in stone; mistakes do happen; systems are fallible, professors and administrators are human, and you do count.

> **Ultimately, your success depends on you. Think of yourself as an informed and valued consumer. You have made choices and sacrifices to come to this university, and you intend to make your investment worthwhile.**

The key is to become your own advocate...

- **Ask for what you need...** and if your problem is course-related, start with the Teaching Assistant. If the TA can't or doesn't help, talk to the professor. In extreme circumstances, you may need to continue up the ladder and contact the Department Head, the Dean of the Faculty, or, if necessary, the President.
- **Challenge your assigned grade...** if you have excellent reason to believe you were unfairly evaluated. Make an appointment to talk with your professor. Bring concrete examples or evidence, including specific references to textbooks or articles. Be prepared to explain your point of view rationally.
- **Ask how you can improve...** if you are not earning the grade you want or need. What can you do, in addition to tests and assignments, to improve your mark? Perhaps additional study assignments are an option.
- **Ask for an extension...** to complete an assignment, if you really need one. Don't be frivolous about time. You can safely assume that your professor has heard every imaginable excuse at least once, and usually from a better actor than you!
- **Suggest an alternative solution...** to your concern or problem, and ask for your professor's input. Do what you can to be proactive and solution-oriented. You want help, not rescuing.

Being your own advocate applies to more than academia. It also applies to friends, peers, fellow students, and dates. As is true anywhere, dangerous things sometimes happen on university campuses. Pay attention to student affairs and security warnings about unsafe places on campus, be smart about drugs and alcohol (date rape drugs are particularly scary right now), and listen to your own intuition.

- **Act with respect for yourself and others...** Hold your tears and your tantrums. Be clear, logical, flexible and open to suggestion. Maturity in your approach will encourage others to treat you seriously and with respect.
- **Be sure you have followed instructions...** and completed requirements, before asking for help (unless there are extenuating circumstances). This is your education. You are accountable.
- **Be realistic in your expectations...** and know that you may not always get all your requests or needs met. At least you will have tried!

To students with special needs...
(Please read this, even if you think it doesn't apply to you.)

Many students have special needs that limit their access to everyday resources. Some require special resources or assistance to make student life meaningful and successful. If this is you, remember you must ask for what you need. Start by doing your research early! Will the universities you are interested in be willing and able to accommodate you? Is there an office responsible to support students with special needs? What can they do on your behalf?

Most campus buildings are now accessible to wheelchairs and walking aids, although many could still be greatly improved. If you have a vision or hearing impairment, you need to consult your teachers. Professors are usually happy to have your seeing-eye dog become a regular class member, or to use the amplification device you provide, or to allow you to record lectures. They must, however be asked!

Some of you will have learning needs that are not easily defined. You may have been assessed as having attention deficit disorder (ADD), or perhaps dyslexia. You might experience difficulty learning in a traditional classroom environment. Perhaps you have a problem with reading. Whatever the situation, *don't be discouraged*. Remember, you have found useful strategies which enabled you to get this far.

There are always possibilities and solutions...

- Become your own advocate. (Go back and re-read the last two pages.) Ask for what you need to succeed. You are a consumer!
- Assume that your requests are as legitimate as anyone else's. You don't need to accept "no" or "wait." Keep asking until you find someone who will respond.
- Develop your problem-solving skills. If one strategy doesn't work, try another. Ask yourself, "What do I need to do to fix this?"
- Become part of a special needs group, or start one of your own. There is strength in numbers. 'Squeaky wheels' get attention!
- Build a strong support network to help you advocate and problem-solve. Use your network to vent, brainstorm, practice strategies, and celebrate victories.

Some typical student requests...
- Extra exam time, or oral exams.
- Recording a lecture.
- Having an aide take notes.
- A separate room for taking tests.
- Copies of the instructor's notes.
- A private facility to rest and change feeding tubes or catheters.
- A temporary ramp to access the classroom.

Do the best you can to take care of yourself.
You deserve it!

Our vision for you:

A
Fulfilling
Rewarding
Energizing
Post-Secondary
Education.

Good Luck!!

appendix:

Extra
Smarts

*everything else we'd
like you to know...*

Welcome to Canada (or we look forward to welcoming you soon)! Canadian universities are actively recruiting international students. Some universities work with recruiting representatives who travel internationally. Others facilitate the long-distance registration process with fax lines and e-mail. Many schools offer extra support through English-as-a-second-language (ESL) programs, special social activities, help lines, buddy systems, and accommodation arrangements. As you evaluate different universities, investigate the facilities available for international students — they can make a big difference to your learning experience.

As an international student, you will pay non-resident tuition fees, which are approximately five times higher than the fees Canadian students pay. Even at that, your fees are usually much less than international tuition fees in the United States, and often not much more than you would pay at home.

Moving to another country can, of course, be difficult. You will probably be coping with a foreign language, a different culture, strange customs, home-sickness, and sometimes discrimination or prejudice. Yet 33,000 international students come to Canada every year! If you plan to study in Canada, be prepared to spend plenty of time and energy on your application process. You need to start early.

Applying to Canadian Universities...
Before Canadian immigration authorities will grant you a student visa, you must be officially admitted to a university. There are no standard admission procedures. Each university sets its own. Don't assume that information you receive from one university is applicable to another.

Information on Canadian universities is available at education centres set up in Canadian Embassies in Taiwan, South Korea, Thailand, Hong Kong, Singapore, Malaysia, Indonesia and in India, as well as Europe and Britain. You can also write directly to any Canadian university. If you connect to the *Maclean's* online

D

directory, you can link to all Canadian university home pages.
(http://www.canoe.co/macleans/pipeline/unimag/directory.html)

If you are applying to attend a university in Ontario, all your correspondence should be sent to:

> The Ontario Universities Application Centre
> P.O. Box 1328
> Guelph, Ontario, Canada N1H 7P4
> Phone: (519) 823-1940
> Internet: http://ouainfo.ouac.on.ca

All other university applications and documents should be mailed to the Registrar's Office at your chosen universities.

Although there are no standardized entrance tests for undergraduate students, you will need to provide academic records, official high school and university or college transcripts, and certified translations into English (if the documents are in a language other than English or French). You will also need to write the TOEFL, if your home language is not English. Normally, transcripts are sent directly from your graduating school to the Canadian universities where you are applying. Check with each university about specific requirements.

Dealing with the Canadian Government...

The Canadian government requires all prospective international students to apply for Student Authorization. Normally, you are granted authorization for the length of your university program (bachelor's degree, master's degree or doctorate). Student Authorization forms are available at Canadian Embassies, Consulates and High Commissions. Some of you may also require a student visa, particularly if you come from India, China Thailand, or other Asian countries.

Before you are authorized as a student and given a visa, you may be interviewed by the Department of Citizenship and Immigration. If so, be sure to have the following documents handy:

- an acceptance letter from a Canadian university;
- an outline of the length of your program, provided by your university;

- official proof from your bank of sufficient funds to cover all your tuition and book expenses, as well as about $10,000 CDN per year for living costs;
- a medical certificate from an approved physician indicating your good health status; and
- a valid passport.

You can transfer to another university under your student authorization, provided you do not increase the length of your stay or change the status of your program. To do that, you require further authorization from the immigration processing centre in Vegreville, Alberta. (The International Students Office at your university or college can give you the address.) Be sure to notify the immigration authorities of *any change in your status.*Concealing this information will result in your expulsion from Canada.

If you plan to study in Quebec, you will also need approval from the Quebec Provincial Government. Write to them at:

> Quebec Immigration Service
> 365 rue Ste Catherine ouest (5e Ètage)
> Montreal, Quebec, Canada H3B 1A4

English or French Language Requirements...
Canadian universities and colleges expect you to demonstrate proficiency in English (or French, if you plan to attend a French-speaking university or college), before you are accepted. TOEFL (Test of English as a Foreign Language) is the most widely-used and accepted proficiency test. You can take the necessary preparation courses at colleges, universities and private language schools. TOEFL exams are offered at language-testing centres world-wide, and are available each month. Minimum acceptable test scores vary; you may need to take the exam several times. You can get information, practice tests and registration forms from:

> Test of English as a Foreign Language (TOEFL)
> Educational Testing Service
> Princeton, New Jersey, U.S.A. 08540

Making your living arrangements...
A new country can be bewildering and stressful. You want your living arrangements to be as welcoming as possible. Living in university residence with other students may

ease the stress, loneliness and confusion of being so far away from home. Universities will send you information on the available options and costs. Some of you, on the other hand, may feel more at ease living with a host family — at least until you feel more at home in Canada. Information on accommodation alternatives is available from university housing offices, or from the International Student Centre at the university of your choice. Another option is to share accommodation with other students off campus. In that case, be prepared that landlords may want to check your credit rating or previous accommodation history, to be sure you pay your rent.

Working as a Student...

Work for international students is usually restricted to on-campus jobs, on a part-time basis during the school year, and on a full-time basis in the summer. If you are enrolled in a co-op program, you can work off campus, as long as you provide a letter from your Department to the authorities. As a graduate student, you can accept a university position as a Graduate Teaching Assistant. After graduation, you can apply for permission to work in Canada for up to 12 months, in a position directly related to your field of study, provided you start work within 60 days of receiving notification of obtaining your degree.

If you are married, your partner is allowed to work anywhere in Canada, if he or she has received employment authorization from Citizenship and Immigration Canada.

Make sure you have Health Insurance...

Rules for health insurance differ for each province. International students in Alberta, British Columbia and Saskatchewan are covered by the provincial health insurance plans. (There is no charge for this plan in Saskatchewan. In Alberta and British Columbia, you will pay about $35 per month.) All other provinces require you to buy health insurance from private insurers, at rates of approximately $370 to $500 per year. At some universities, health insurance premiums are included in your registration fees. Check to make sure! It is important that you register with the provincial insurance plan when you arrive. Without adequate health insurance, you will face extremely high medical costs if you become ill or need to use health care facilities.

Hanna and Asif came from Palestine to study in Canada. As a young, newly-married couple, they decided to find accommodation with a Canadian family who would help them adjust to life in Canada, and also respect their need for privacy. They found a basement suite close to the college, and soon became good friends with their landlords upstairs. In return for some additional practice in English conversation, Hanna and Asif offered to do some child care, and clean the house each week. After a year, they moved into their own apartment, but they stayed friends with the family who had helped them feel welcome in Canada.

Visiting the United States from Canada...

Many of you will want to visit the United States for at least a weekend while you are in Canada. To do that, you will need a tourist visa. It is a really good idea to apply for a tourist visa for the United States from your home country before you leave for Canada. Sometimes the U.S. Embassy or Consulate will issue you a tourist visa from Canada, but often they will not! Be prepared. Have your visas and other international documents with you when you arrive in Canada.

Finding further information...

An International Student's Handbook is available at:
> The Canadian Bureau for International Education
> 220 Laurier Avenue W., Suite 1100
> Ottawa, Ontario, Canada K1P 5Z9

Other useful sources include:
> Association of Universities and Colleges of Canada
> 350 Albert Street
> Ottawa, Ontario, Canada K1R 1B1
> Internet: http://www.aucc.ca

> Council of Ministers of Education, Canada
> 252 Bloor Street W., Suite 5-200
> Toronto, Ontario, Canada M5S 1V5

D

Mature students, most professors will tell you, tend to be keen, excellent, interested participants in their education. Given all the demands on a mature student's time — work and/or children being just two of the more common — this is something of a paradox. Research shows that mature students are attentive, goal-oriented and strategic about working smart. Most have enough life experience to know what they want. So if you are heading back to school after some time away, take heart. You have high potential to succeed!

We have written *College Smarts™* to students of all ages, and we hope you find all of it useful. Here are a few extra tips especially for you. Take what you like and leave the rest!

A Balancing Act in Progress: Work and School...
Many of you will need to work while you are at school. Plan your schedule to avoid overload as much as possible. You may find our sections on working while at school, as well as those dealing with schedules, study tips and time management, particularly relevant. Our information on choosing a college/university, and student financing, may also save you time and research.

The Toughest Piece: Children and School...
Many students have families who need time, care and love. Include family members in your planning, and be as realistic about your (and their) expectations as possible. You will need precise scheduling, an ability to live with reduced sleep and recreation, and a willingness to accept help from others to make this work.

You may find it appropriate to start your study program on a part-time basis. There are several immediate advantages. Fewer classes mean greater flexibility to accommodate family needs, and part-time study is less expensive. If you decide to study full-time, you will probably find yourself making major adjustments to your lifestyle and to your family's. They may protest and complain at first, because you will be less available. Don't give up! Most families don't die from adjusting. They thrive! You may also need careful budgeting — or a creative class schedule — to accommodate day-care or out-of-school care for younger children.

Guilt is a *big issue* for many parents returning to school. Practice letting go of some responsibilities, and allowing others to take them over. Don't do for your kids what they can do for themselves! Some of your study time can become family time. You are setting a great example as you settle down to do your assignments, while your children are doing theirs. *Keep talking to your family* about what you are doing, learning, needing, and feeling. Listen carefully. If your communication channels are open, you are halfway there.

As you stretch and grow, you'll discover a great sense of accomplishment. Reach for your dreams! Success will be yours!

Summer programs for high school students...
For those of you who have the good fortune to consider a challenging summer school option, here is a small selection of the programs available in Canada, the United States, and internationally. The programs are often expensive; ask about available scholarships.

1. Sample Summer Programs In Canada...
Deep River Science Academy
National Registrar @ Box 600, Deep River, Ontario K0J 1P0
Phone: (613) 584-4541
        1-800-760-DRSA
Fax: (613) 584-9597
e-mail: DRSA@intranet.ca
Internet: http://intranet.ca/~drsa/
These science and engineering programs are offered in Deep River, Ontario, as well as in Kelowna, British Columbia and Pinawa, Manitoba. The programs offer six weeks of research participation in a stimulating environment, geared to students with strong grades and an interest in science and engineering. The current cost is $3,700 inclusive. You can apply for bursaries.

Shad Valley Summer Program
Canadian Centre for Creative Technology
8 Young Street East, Waterloo, Ontario N2J 2L3
Phone: (519) 884-8844
Fax: (519) 884-8191
Internet: http://www.shads.org/
The criteria for this program include high grades, especially in Math and Sciences, as well as initiative, motivation, creativity, and the ability to get along well with people. This four-week engineering and entrepreneurship opportunity is offered at various universities across the country, from Nova Scotia to British Columbia. Apply by December for the following summer.

2. Sample Summer Programs in the United States...

Carleton College Summer Writing Program

Office of Summer Academic Programs
Northfield, Minnesota, USA 55057
Phone: (507) 663-4038
Internet: http://www.Carleton.EDU/
For those of you who love to write — spend three weeks at this top liberal arts college, with students from all over the world, learning to develop and polish your writing skills.

Harvard University Summer School
Secondary School Program

51 Brattle Street
Cambridge, Massachusetts, USA 02138-3722
Phone: (617) 495-3193
Experience a taste of life at Harvard: choose from a wide range of academic courses in the Sciences, Arts, Humanities, Fine Arts, Social Sciences; play in the Summer School Orchestra or Pops Band; live in residence. You can also attend a college fair, do some career planning, and visit other colleges in New England.

Operation Catapult
Rose-Hulman Institute of Technology

5500 Wabash Avenue
Terre Haute, Indiana, USA 47803-9959
Phone: (812) 877-1511 Extension 8210
Internet: http://www.rose-hulman.edu/
The criteria for selection here are quite stringent. This is an exciting three-week program for those of you interested in a chemistry, physics, engineering or math career. You will need good scores on the PSAT exam — check with your school counsellor about taking the test.

3. Sample Summer Programs Internationally:

AS Interculture Canada

1231 St. Catherine Street West, Suite 505
Montreal, Quebec H3G 1P5
Phone: (514) 288-3282
    1-800-361-7248 (Eastern Canada)
    1-800-361-1879 (Newfoundland and Western Canada)
Spend the summer as an International Exchange Student, living with a host family in any one of twenty or more countries.

EF International Language Schools
60 Bloor St. West, Suite 405
Toronto, Ontario M4W 3B8
Phone: (416) 323-0330
Fax: (416) 927-8664.
          1-800-387-1463
If you are seeking cultural and language immersion in Spanish, Italian, German and French, this program offers two-week consecutive modules which increase in difficulty as you proceed. Take one or several modules in Europe, over the summer.

Study in Oxford and/or France with Peel Board of Education Community Education, Summer Programs
160 Traders Boulevard E., Suite 114
Mississauga, Ontario L4Z 3K7
Phone: (905) 568-1080 Extension 230
Fax: (905) 568-4690
Internet: http://www.comed.on.ca/

Blyth & Company Travel, Summer Programs
13 Hazelton Avenue
Toronto, Ontario M5R 2E1
Phone: 1-800-964-3416 (Ontario)
          1-800-387-1387 (Rest of Canada)
Fax: (416) 964-3416.
If you have dreamed of studying at Oxford University, this is an opportunity to take credit courses in English Literature, Media, Creative Writing, Art History, Business Studies and much more. You can also travel to the south of France to study photography and French. If you prefer, you can combine the two programs and visit both England and France.

International Learning Programs for High School Graduates...

Sea Education Association
P.O. Box 6, Woods Hole, Massachusetts
USA 02543
Phone: (508) 540-3954
Fax: (508) 457-4673.
This program accepts some high school graduates. Participants spend four weeks at sea as part of the research team, and four weeks studying oceanography, pollution and marine ecosystems through labs, fieldtrips and classes.

AFS Interculture Canada
1231 St. Catherine Street West, Suite 505
Montreal, Quebec H3G 1P5
Phone: (514) 288-3282
      1-800-361-7248 (Eastern Canada)
      1-800-361-1879 (Newfoundland and Western Canada)
These international exchange programs run from six months (in Costa Rica and Argentina) to a year (in many other countries). Choose an exchange in Australia, Japan, Thailand, Argentina, Bolivia, Brazil, Chile, Ecuador or Costa Rica. You live with a host family, attend school, and have the opportunity to become fluent in another language, while experiencing a different culture.

Lycée Canadien en France
13 Hazelton Avenue
Toronto, Ontario M5R 2E1
Phone: (416) 926-0828
        1-800-387-5603 (Ontario)
        1-800-387-1387 (Rest of Canada)
Fax: (416) 964-3416.
This program will appeal to students learning French. Be prepared for a strong academic focus, and expectations that you be independent and self-motivated. Students can choose to stay with a family or at the school.

D

Neuchatel Junior College

330 Bay Street
Toronto, Ontario M5H 2S8
Phone:(416) 368-8169
        1-800-263-2923
e-mail: info@neuchatel.org
Living with French-speaking families, you will participate in a program which is academically challenging and culturally exciting. Part of the attraction is the opportunity to travel through Europe, as a complement to your school work.

Canadian College Italy

59 Macamo Ct.
Maple, Ontario L6A 1G1
Phone:(905) 508-7108
        1-800-422-0548
Fax: (905) 508-5480
e-mail: staff@cci.lanciano.ch.it
Internet: http://web.idirect.com/~cci/
This is a co-ed school in Lanciano, with a traditional academic focus. The school boasts excellent science labs and small classes. Opportunities also exist for chaperoned, supervised travel in Italy and the rest of Europe.

United World Colleges

London House, Mecklenburgh Square
London, UK WC1N 2AB
Phone:(44 171) 833-2626
Fax: (44 171) 837-3102
e-mail: uwcio@gn.apc.org
http://owlnet.rice.edu/~walkerb/uwc/uwchome/html
The United World Colleges are an international consortium of colleges with nine campuses in different countries. The Colleges offer two year programs, which promote opportunities for you to learn and experience peace, personal challenge and cooperation, while preparing for the International Baccalaureate exams. You can choose to study in Canada (at Lester B. Pearson College on Vancouver Island, British Columbia) or at a college in Italy, Switzerland, Wales, Swaziland (Southern Africa), Singapore, Venezuela, Norway, or Hong Kong.

Katimavik
2065 Rue Parthenais, Suite 405
Montreal, Quebec H2K 3T1
Phone: (514) 525-1503
        1-888-525-1503 (toll free)
Fax: (514) 525-1953.
The Canadian Government established Katimavik in the 1970s, to give young Canadians work experience. Funding restrictions closed the program for many years, but it was re-established in 1995. Students aged 17 to 21 live and work in small groups in three different regions of Canada, contributing to non-profit projects and developing fluency in either English or French. This is a 7 to 8 month program.

French For Non-Francophones (FNF)
Laval University, Quebec
Summer Language Bursary Program
Phone: (403) 427-5539
e-mail: senechaf@sfb.aecd.gov.ab.ca
A five-week language immersion program for students from Canada, the United States, Mexico and South America gives you the opportunity to enhance your French, become acquainted with Quebec and meet students from other countries. French classes are held by day, evenings and weekends are spent in workshops, sports, travel, the arts, and socializing. You do not need to have much knowledge of French in order to participate. Some bursaries are available.

Canada World Youth
10816A - 82 Avenue, Suite 205
Edmonton, Alberta T6E 2B3
Phone: (403) 432-1877
Fax: (403) 433-4489
e-mail: cwy@cwy.ca
*An international exchange program matches successful
applicants between 17 and 20 years of age with other
students from Canada and abroad. The first three months
of the program are spent in a Canadian community, working
and learning to fundraise. The next four months are spend
abroad with a supervised host family. Each group of students
is encouraged to participate in the community in which
they live. The mission is to create opportunities for people
to participate actively and meaningfully in the development
of "just, harmonious and sustainable societies." Exchange
students are placed in Asia, Africa, Latin America and
the Caribbean.*

Distance Learning Programs in Canada...

Athabasca University
Box 10,000
Athabasca, Alberta T9S 1A1
Phone:(403) 675-6434
Fax: (403) 675-6174
e-mail: reginfo@cs.athabascau.ca
Internet: http://www.athabascau.ca

British Columbia Open University
c/o Open Learning Agency
P.O. Box 82080
Burnaby, British Columbia V5C 6J8
Phone:(604) 431-3000
        1-800-633-1663 (Toll free in B.C.)
e-mail: studentserv@ola.bc.ca
Internet: http://www.ola.bc.ca

The following universities also
offer some distance learning programs:

University of Waterloo Correspondence Program
University of Waterloo
Waterloo, Ontario N2L 3G1
Phone: (519) 888-4050
e-mail: distance@corr1.uwaterloo.ca
Internet:
http://www.adm.uwaterloo.ca/infoded/de&ce.html

Queens University
Admissions Office (Part-time Studies)
Kingston, Ontario K7L 2N6
Phone: (613) 545-2218

University of Windsor
Division of Continuing Studies
Windsor, Ontario N9B 3P4
Phone:(519) 253-4232 (Ext. 3470) or
        1-800-263-1242 (Toll free)
Fax: (519) 973-7038

Wilfrid Laurier University
Office of the Registrar
75 University Avenue W
Waterloo, Ontario N2L 3C5
Phone: (519) 884-0710 (Ext. 3378)
Fax: (519) 884-8826.

Lakehead University
Distance Education, Regional Centre, Room RC 0009
Thunder Bay, Ontario P7B 5E1
Phone: (807) 346-7730
Fax: (807) 343-8008.

Some Places to Look (mostly on the Internet) for Student Loans and Scholarships...

Canada Student Loans Program
http://schoolnet2.carleton.ca/English/ext/gov/stud_loans

Canadian Scholarships on File — CD ROM
Phone: 1-800-563-0331
Fax: (204) 453-7169
e-mail: rebecca@cdnscholars.com
Canadian Scholarships on File provides a questionnaire to match you with appropriate scholarships, based on your academic standing, proposed program of study, residence, gender, ethnic background, and so on. You can then apply for those scholarships that interest you. (Check with your Guidance Counsellors at school. They may be interested in ordering a CD ROM for their resources.)

Scholarship Websites
www.fastweb.com Click on: FASTWEB Canada - a database for financial aid, to match you with available rewards, and a mailbox, to keep you up to date. www.collegenet.com Click on: CollegeNet Match 25

Parents Guide
http://www.parentsguide.com/ Use this site to access the data base from Canadian Scholarships on File (a CD ROM offering). You can answer the scholarship questionnaire provided to you, without having to purchase the CD ROM. The CD ROM data is included for your information.

Some great examples of what's available...

Canada Trust Scholarships for Outstanding Community Leadership

Canada Trust Scholarship Program
161 Bay Street, P.O. Box 19003, Stn BRM B
Toronto, Ontario M7Y 3M3

$40,000 over four years, for students with outstanding community service.

Canadian Merit Scholarship Foundation Awards

Canadian Merit Scholarship Foundation
R.R. 1, Wellington, Ontario K0K 3L0

$14,000 plus four years tuition, for strong leadership and community service.

Terry Fox Humanitarian Award

Terry Fox Humanitarian Award Program
Simon Fraser University
Burnaby, B.C. V5A 1S6

$16,000 over four years, for personal courage and community service.

For information and practice tests, contact Educational Testing Services (ETS) at: ETS NET www.ets.org/ or Kaplan at www.kaplan.com. Kaplan offers an online SAT prep course and interaction with instructors.

If you are applying to undergraduate programs in the United States ...writing the SAT (Scholastic Aptitude Test) or the ACT (American College Test)

If your desired institution requires an SAT or ACT score, we suggest you start preparing early! These tests require a different approach to test-taking than you may be used to from high school. The key is to be a smart, strategic test-taker. You need to understand how the tests work, and know what format to expect. There are good study guides available — we strongly suggest you use them! Try some practice tests; your results will give you a good sense of how much extra study time you need. Practice definitely produces higher test scores.

Our basic tips...

- Standardized test results are based on the number of items you answer correctly in the time allowed, regardless of the difficulty of individual questions. Your goal is simply to answer as many questions correctly as possible.
- Time is always tight in standardized tests. Strategic time management makes a big difference.
- Learn the instructions from practice tests — they are always the same. That way you won't have to waste time reading instructions during the exam.
- Test questions are always arranged from easy to difficult. Answer the easy ones first.
- Circle the questions you don't know. Come back to them later if you have time.
- Fill out the answer sheets carefully. Make sure you are marking the right spot for each question.
- Pause to think before you answer. Beware of distractors — those answers that appear correct at first glance. Decide on your answer and then find it among the choices offered.
- Guess if you don't know. Guessing right will gain you points; guessing wrong will lose you points. However, if you eliminate the obviously wrong choices, you have a good chance to guess right from the remaining ones.
- Maintain a steady pace. You have a lot of questions to answer in a short time. Keep your brain and eyes moving. Don't get blocked on any one item.

D

THE ADVENTURES OF GRADUATE SCHOOL

Whether you are heading for graduate school as soon as you complete your degree, or you plan to work for a few years and then return to the world of academia, here are our hints to smooth the way. The basic principles will be familiar; they are similar to what you have already learned.

Start planning to qualify early... You need to maintain a high GPA (3.5 or better), particularly in your last two years of undergraduate work.

Research your options... At the graduate level, specialization is the key to choosing a school. You need to know where the good programs are. Consult graduate school directories, advisors, and the Internet. Most graduate school applications must be submitted by February of the year you plan to attend. Start your research a year before that deadline.

Check with professional associations... Consult provincial and national associations in your chosen field, as well as their American counterparts, for lists of approved schools. Not all programs are equal, and not all are approved. This is especially important if you plan to study in the United States or abroad. Be sure that you can be licensed in Canada (in your chosen province) and/or in the United States, depending on where you want to work.

Collect application packages... The Graduate School office may provide general application information, while your chosen department provides customized program information and requirements. You may need to apply to both the Graduate Studies Program and the Department — be sure to double-check. When you are ready to submit applications, use forms from the current year.

Read and compare carefully... Narrow your selection to those schools that will meet your needs, and whose criteria you fit best. Consider the program reputation, as well as location, cost, length, and prerequisite courses.

For those of you who dread the Standardized Tests – prepare ahead, take the test and stop worrying. In the grand scheme of things, these scores are usually given less weight than your GPA, essay, references and interviews

Take the necessary admission tests... Professional programs often require you to take a specialized admission test—the GMAT for an MBA, the LSAT for Law, the MCAT for medicine. You may also need to take the GRE (Graduate Record Examinations). We encourage you to take your test early, preferably a full year before you intend to enroll. You need time to prepare, and you need time to rewrite the test if you are disappointed with your score. You also need six to eight weeks between taking the test and getting the results to the schools you have selected. Be prepared! Know what format to expect, and practice on sample questions and mock exams. Check the Internet for samples. You can take the GRE by computer at selected centres.

Prepare your essay or 'letter of intent...' Read the directions! Each school has its own requirements. Some are specific (i.e. 350 words, double-spaced); others are more general. Don't get your application shredded because you ignored instructions.

Request your transcripts... You will need official transcripts from your graduating university, and from any other institutions you attended to earn your degree. To be official, transcripts must be sent directly from your university to the graduate school(s) where you are applying - they cannot pass through your hands. Check for deadlines.

Prepare all your applications at once... Christmas break is a good time for this task. That way you can concentrate on your final winter semester, knowing that all your applications are on their way.

Research and apply for scholarships and loans... Scholarship deadlines are often in February. Apply even if you do not completely fit the criteria - sometimes scholarship money is not awarded because no one applied. Federal and provincial student loan forms are usually available at your university's Awards and Financial Services Office by late April.

If you plan to study in the United States... You will need to offer proof that you have sufficient funds to pay for your entire program, including tuition, books, living expenses, and travel. "Proof" may include documentation from your bank, from the Student Finance Board in your home province, and/or from your financial sponsors (parents or relatives). Without this documentation, you will not get a student visa from the American government. Your school will send you the relevant forms to complete. (Note that you will be paying non-resident tuition fees, which can be five times the tuition paid by state residents.)

Keep copies of every document you send... We also recommend you send all correspondence by double-registered mail or courier. Take no chances!

Be prepared to spend some money... Each institution will require an application fee of about $30 to $50. Universities in the United States and overseas will cost more, and will require payment in the appropriate currency. (Money orders are a good idea here.) Transcripts will also cost you money, as will copying, couriers, and mail.

About the all-important reference letters ...

- Most graduate programs require letters of reference from at least two professors, and sometimes a third letter from someone you worked for (as a volunteer or in a summer job) in a field related to your degree.
- Request references from professors who know your specialty. Get to know your professors, and become known to them. Ask questions, discuss assignments, show your interest. (Be careful, however, not to abuse their time.)
- Approach the professors you have chosen in September or October of the year before your applications are due. Ask if the professor is willing to write a good reference letter on your behalf. There is no point in soliciting a mediocre letter; it will likely work against you.
- If the professor says yes, provide a package of information about you — your current resume; a record of all your courses/grades/GPA; a list of courses taken and grades received from this professor (include copies of papers or assignments); an overview of your personal interests, strengths, and weaknesses; and a statement about why you want to continue your education.

Although law school admission is extremely competitive, some faculties - including those at University of Calgary and University of Windsor - believe that maturity, community involvement, and work/life experience are at least as important as grades and LSAT scores. As the University of Windsor law program proclaims: "We aren't looking for the best test scores, we're looking for the best people."

- The professor will also need the reference forms required by each university you are applying to. Complete the necessary background information about you on each form, to save your professor some time and make this as easy as possible.
- Be clear about your application deadlines. Ask for the reference letter to be completed by January — and offer a gentle prompt in December. This is probably not the most critical thing on your professor's calendar! Say thank you when the letter is done. A personal card or a small gift is usually appropriate. Everyone likes to be acknowledged!
- You can waive the right to read the reference letters submitted on your behalf. If you waive this right, you demonstrate your confidence that the reference is supportive. This looks good to your desired school. Give your professor a stamped, pre-addressed envelope to each school to expedite the mailing process. Ask her or him to enclose the letter, seal the envelope, and sign the seal. You can then collect and mail the envelopes yourself. (Again, double-registered mail or courier is a good idea.)

Admission Criteria for Graduate and Professional Schools...

Graduate schools select students on the basis of:
- Grade point average
- Graduate essay or letter of intent
- Reference letters
- Standardized test scores (GRE, LSAT, MCAT, and so on)
- Personal experience and (sometimes) an interview.

Typically, each member of the Graduate Selection Committee reviews the portfolio of each applicant. Applicants are ranked based on grades, references, achievements, volunteer and work experience, and stated goals. (Career-related volunteer and work experience have become crucial factors in the selection process for many programs.) Committee members may also assess your compatibility with the demands of the program, your "well-roundedness," and your capacity to bring unique gifts and talents to the department. When the selection committee meets, each candidate is evaluated once more and the final selection is made. A wait list is also prepared.

D

Your acceptance (or rejection) letters should arrive beginning in April. If you are placed on a wait list, you stand a good chance of acceptance but you may not hear until late July or August. Each school has its own schedule. Usually, you have somewhere between ten days and three weeks to respond to an offer. Prioritize schools in order of your preference, and accept or reject accordingly. If you are accepted to your third and sixth choices in one week, accept number three and reject number six. If you are then accepted to your first choice, go back and reject all the rest. Once you have rejected an offer, you can't change your mind — your spot will have been given to someone else. (You can always accept first and reject later, making someone on the wait list very happy!)

Don't immediately reject any school that is not your first choice, because your first choice might reject you! Some schools will extend your acceptance deadline (if you ask), and some will let you know where you stand (if you call and let them know you've been accepted elsewhere). If they really want you, and they know you have been accepted elsewhere, they'll send an offer in short order!

About the Authors' Work

Catherine and Ron Dougan are co-owners of the Career Institute of Calgary. Their expertise in career planning is offered through speaking engagements and workshop facilitation, as well as individual coaching.

To share your feedback on College Smarts™, or to book the Dougans for a speaking engagement or their Career Smarts™ Workshop, contact:

The Career Institute of Calgary
1407 - 2 Street S.W.
Calgary, Alberta, Canada T2R 0W7
Phone: (403) 263-5237
Fax: (403) 283-0719
E-mail: CIC@career-smarts.com

Visit us!
http://www.college-smarts.com.
In addition to a wealth of information, the **College Smarts™ website provides access to every university and college website in Canada.** Use College Smarts™ as a gateway to exploration!